FPCC

JAN 2 8 1992

INVENTORY 98

St. Louis Community College

Forest Park
Florissant Valley
Meramec

Instructional Resources
St. Louis, Missouri

THE SENSE OF STYLE

THE SENSE OF STYLE

Reading English Prose

James Thorpe

Archon Books
1987

Printed in the United States of America

The paper used in this publication meets the minimum requirements
of American National Standard for Information Sciences—Permanence
of Paper for Printed Library Materials, ANSI Z39.48–1984. ∞

Set in Baskerville by
Brevis Press, Bethany, Connecticut
Designed by Patricia Larsen Barratt

Library of Congress Cataloging-in-Publication Data

Thorpe, James Ernest, 1915–
    The sense of style.
    Includes index.
    1. English prose literature—History and criticism.
    2. English language—Style.   I. Title.
PR751.T46   1987   828'.08   87–17498
ISBN 0–208–02181–7 (alk. paper)

CONTENTS

THE WRITER TO THE READER

Dear Reader,

I enjoyed writing this book. I hope that you get a good return from reading it. I'd like to tell you, before you get started, a little about what I'm trying to do.

Language is man's most exquisite invention. Yet, at its best, language may transmit only an incomplete understanding of any moderately complex communication. And so we are always fooling around with words to see if we can make them do more for us. Or to see whether we can get by with less effort in our dealings with words. At the same time, the needs and ambitions that animate us are constantly in a state of flux. Whatever we do, we always reflect our selves as we try to come to terms with language.

Stop right there! The paragraph you just finished reading: you did notice that the style changed, didn't you? The first two sentences were (I thought) rather formal, abstract, perhaps a little stiff. Then there was an abrupt shift to informality, like talking to a friend for two sentences, and then back to a more formal manner for the last two sentences.

You may have been puzzled by these shifts, and assumed that they were simply caused by ineptness. Or you may have been offended by the didactic tone, or doubtful about the sentiments that were being expressed with such a show of confidence. If so, we were making a start, however unpromising, in forming a relationship between you and me, in this case between the reader and the writer.

On the other hand, suppose that (honestly) you really didn't notice the shifts in style, or at least didn't pay much attention to them while waiting for something really memorable to be said. In most reading, we do move right along, alert to main points, trying to grasp the key ideas. The way we have to deal with the great quantities of written matter set before us in newspapers, magazines, memos, appeals, ads, and so forth. In those cases, the role of language sometimes diminishes to the task of giving information or making a case or getting our attention long enough to communicate a simple message. Since we are bombarded by so much written and spoken language in our daily lives, we have to defend ourselves against the invasion of our intellectual privacy by blocking out what is more than we want to deal with.

It is mainly because of the need for self-protection against a deluge of verbal material (much of which we dismiss as trash, garbage, junk) that literate people in Western society read with less close attention to the text (I think) than they used to do. Less than fifty or a hundred years ago, and less than at any time since the ability to read began to be moderately widespread, some five hundred years ago.

Too bad, but probably necessary. The choice is skimming, summary, condensation on the one hand, or (on the other hand) the discipline of very rigorous selectivity. Mostly we have chosen the former way. Once we put up our guard against some forms of language, we never quite take it down all the way, except with a conscious effort that we are rarely willing to make. So the loss is almost everywhere.

Books of literary study are books about reading in the sense that they try to help us, in one way or another, to come to terms with (that is, read) a text or a lot of texts. The thought that keeps coming back most often in this book is the relation between reading and performance. Reading a text aloud to an audience is a performance in the obvious sense. But silent reading is performance also, with the external manifestations kept inside. So throughout this book I keep thinking of reading and performance as parallel terms. Reading and performance both lead to our understanding of texts, and they are also the signs of the way in which we do in fact understand texts. (Of course it is only reading aloud that reveals the signs to an outsider.) In this pattern, understanding is the term I use for what we are trying to achieve in dealing with texts.

This is a book about the sense of style in expository prose. Although the derivation of poetry from song was a long way back, the family resemblance is still sometimes visible. Prose, expository prose, does not have such a grand progenitor. It is sometimes pushed into the company of poetry as a visiting cousin from the country, but its direct ancestors are really people talking to one another, asking and answering questions, explaining things, discussing their lives and their ideas and their loves, expounding their feelings and their beliefs. A lot of clean-up work had to be done when speech that was oral became prose that was written down. The family resemblance is still sometimes visible, however, even after the faces and hands have all been scrubbed.

Those who live by a hierarchy of kinds or genres may have little regard for expository prose, and think of it as something they hope students will somehow learn to handle somewhere along the line, at least to the point of intelligibility. For the rest of us, it may be the essence of our expressive lives in words, and something that we can never entirely master no matter how much we try or how long we are about it.

So I offer this series of connected studies about reading and understanding expository prose more fully. As you will see, I have been thinking about the sense of style: really the multiplicity of styles that result from different forms of the structural organization of language, and the ways in which these styles affect our understanding. How punctuation indicates structure and guides our understanding, and how historical changes in the conventions of punctuation have altered the structuring of prose and our ways of understanding it. How different arrangements of words within a sentence create different structures and different effects in our understanding. How the rhythm and the sound of words contribute to our sense of structure and to our understanding. How the power of the chosen word interacts with the context of a discourse and affects our understanding. How the relation of the writer and the reader affects our understanding of texts, both in the oral tradition and in the personal and impersonal written tradition. Finally, how we understand a deep meaning of what the text is telling us by interpreting its style.

In this book, I am addressing fellow students of English and American literature. We are all colleagues in the corporate enterprise of the study of literature. I am also addressing all others who have a serious interest in reading expository prose and would like to see whether this book can offer them any useful perceptions about that kind of writing or the kinds of writers discussed. I hope that it can.

The book is full of examples of the work of good writers, and the orientation is literary, not linguistic or philosophical or compositional. I have chosen relatively familiar passages for discussion. The examples are given not to prove an argument but to exemplify a principle. I hope that these passages, and the works of which they are a part, will seem richer from being met in this context.

I have tried hard not to draw too many examples from any single writer or group of writers or age, and the examples run in time from Heraclitus to Samuel Beckett, whatever seemed apt. I hope that the examples are fair, in the sense that each could, in most cases, have a thousand substitutes with no change in the effect of the reasoning. In fact, it was only the exhortation of a friend that led me to leave out about a thousand other wonderful examples.

I had never fully realized, until I was writing this book, how intimately reading and writing are related. Now I see them as reciprocal activities; and in calling them "activities," I mean to stress the active function of each of them. So a study that has to do with reading naturally has also to do with writing, if you look at it from that side.

I was glad to be able to write this book in the cordial environment of the Huntington Library, among many friends. In particular, I have profited from talking with William A. Ringler, Jr., Hallett Smith, and John M. Steadman. Marjorie Perloff generously read everything in its first form and helped me improve it.

I hope that you enjoy the book.

Sincerely,

James Thorpe

1.

SIGNS OF STRUCTURE
Punctuation as Guide to Performance

We get accustomed to convenience without much difficulty. Reading is made simpler by the use of conventional signs that indicate structure and help us to understand a text. We take them for granted and hurry along with our reading.

It has not always been so. In classical antiquity, the words were ordinarily not separated from one another. Moreover, there were essentially no marks of punctuation, no indication of what was a direct quotation, and hardly any devices to set apart sentences or paragraphs or other divisions of a discourse.

The last chapter of Joyce's *Ulysses* gives us a taste of the experience that earlier readers had when they came to deal with a text. Here is a short passage taken from near the end of that last chapter, Molly Bloom's soliloquy. She is musing to herself, silently, about things that had happened to her years before: conversations, acts, thoughts, feelings, reflections. Her musings culminate in recollecting her response to Leopold Bloom's proposal of marriage, and she repeats the word *yes* as a kind of anticipatory chorus of the response that she ultimately gave:

> the sun shines for you he said the day we were lying among the rhododendrons on Howth head in the grey tweed suit and his straw hat the day I got him to propose to me yes first I gave him the bit of seedcake out of my mouth and it was a leapyear like now yes 16 years ago my God after that long kiss I near lost my breath yes he said I was a flower of the mountain yes so we are flowers all a womans body yes that was one true thing he said in his life and the sun shines for you today yes that was why I liked him because I saw he understood or felt what a woman is and I knew I could always get round him

And so on. We cannot simply read these words and let it go at that. The text is never complete. We must always bring something to the text in order to make it usable. A knowledge of the language, of course, the more detailed the better. So far as structure goes: at the least, a sense of pattern so that a structure can be helped to open up as we move along. Preferably, a sense of a multitude of possible patterns, both simple and complex, direct and subtle, and all of their combinations. As well as the experience and tact and taste to see what kind of pattern works best with this particular combination of words. While we read, a sense of structure is developing within us. For those who are inept or inexperienced, our sense of the structure may be crude or illogical or indefensible. Among those who are apt and experienced, the sense of structure may well be somewhat different for different readers, with a defensible argument possible to support each interpretation.

How do we, in fact, read this passage from *Ulysses*? How do we perceive its structure? We have, at best, only rather crude written signs to use in indicating structure. If we wanted to put those same words from *Ulysses* into a conventional form by the use of our ordinary written signs, they might look something like this:

> "The sun shines for you," he said, the day we were lying among the rhododendrons on Howth head, in the grey tweed suit and his straw hat. The day I got him to propose to me. (yes) First, I gave him a bit of seedcake out of my mouth. And it was leapyear, like now. (yes) (16 years ago—my God!) After that long kiss, I near lost my breath. (yes) He said I was a flower of the mountain. (yes) So we are, flowers all, a woman's body. (yes) (That was *one* true thing he said in his life.) And "the sun shines for you today." (yes) That was why I liked him, because I saw he understood (or felt) what a woman *is*. And I knew I could always get round him.

That is one way to read those lines. It is not precisely the way I read them, and probably not exactly the way anyone else reads them, either. Any reading, even a silent reading, depends on features for which we don't have common printing signs, like the kind of intonation, the pitch, the relative emphasis given to different words, the variations in speed and loudness, whether the words are run together or kept apart, and so forth. Not to mention (in the case of reading aloud) gesture and all the other forms of expressiveness that we can use. At least, this second, punctuated version gives some general guidance to the internal structure of the passage.

Maybe we need it and maybe we don't. It may help us to see some details that we might have missed in a quick reading. But it also gives an almost irresistible push toward one kind of understanding. With this kind of punctuation, it would be difficult to feel that the passage is a representation of a stream of consciousness, for example—recollections flowing uninhibited through the memory of a person, now swift, now eddying, now rushing into side channels. Which is, I believe, the effect that Joyce was trying to get us to achieve.

Here is another brief passage for consideration and comparison. It is the very end of that last chapter of *Ulysses*. Molly is thinking about the time, years ago,

> when I put the rose in my hair like the Andalusian girls used or shall I wear a red yes and how he kissed me under the Moorish wall and I thought well as well him as another and then I asked him with my eyes to ask me again yes and then he asked me would I yes to say yes my mountain flower and first I put my arms around him yes and drew him down to me so he could feel my breasts all perfume yes and his heart was going like mad and yes I said yes I will Yes.

Here is a translation of the passage into conventional form, with ordinary punctuation, of Molly's recollection of that time

> when I put the rose in my hair, like the Andalusian girls used. ("Or shall I wear a red?") (yes) And how he kissed me under the Moorish wall, and I thought, "Well, as well him as another." And then I asked him with my eyes to ask again. (yes) And then he asked me would I (yes) to say "Yes." ("My mountain flower!") And first I put my arms around him (yes) and drew him down to me so he could feel my breasts, all perfume. (yes) And his heart was going like mad! And (yes) I said, "Yes, I will—Yes!"

In both passages, the words are exactly the same in the two

versions of each. But the appearance and the response and the effect are different. The first version, with its bare text, gives us all of the verbal signs that we need for reading. The second version, with its guidance of structural signs, comes closer to suggesting what we always do when we read this passage. Or indeed any passage. Whether silently or aloud. . . . That is, we perform it.

Here is another example, from another well-known writer, which will perhaps open the range of the ways we think about punctuation. I present the passage with the exact punctuation that the author used:

> in truth if I should have studied with myself of all points
> of false invections which a poisonous tongue could have
> spit out against that Duke yet would it never have come
> into my head of all other things that any man would: have
> objected want of gentry unto him but this fellow doth like
> him who when he had shot off all his railing quiver called
> one a cuckold that was never married because he would
> not be in debt to any one evil word

The passage is taken from the author's manuscript, written in his own hand. It is not fiction, and not (like the passage from *Ulysses*) an endeavor of art to create an uncommon effect in the reader. It is a straightforward expository essay, part of a defense of the Earl of Leicester, set down about 1585. Only the spelling has been modernized. Notice that the one mark of punctuation that the author used—a colon, about in the middle—would now seem entirely inappropriate at that place.

The author: Sir Philip Sidney. Most modern readers would, I think, be mildly irritated at having to puzzle out the passage in order to perform it. The logic is familiar, and the gist of the meaning is moderately clear. Essentially, we dislike having to make the extra effort to convert rapid reading into expressive performance in order to understand more precisely.

If we were asked to punctuate the passage in something like the way we read and perform it, the passage might look something like this:

> In truth, if I should have studied with myself of all points
> of false invections which a poisonous tongue could have

spit out against that Duke, yet would it never have come
into my head (of all other things) that any man would
have objected want of gentry unto him. But this fellow
doth like him who, when he had shot off all his railing
quiver, called one a cuckold that was never married, because he would not be in debt to any one evil word.

Aside from convenience, what has been gained by this punctuating of the passage? For the deliberate, patient, painstaking
scholar, probably nothing. For the rest of us, the punctuating
brings the passage in from the cold and into the normal conventions that are familiar to us. Within abnormal conventions, we
sometimes feel that we need to be on our guard in case something is being put over on us. The punctuation of the passage
into a familiar form makes the intent and the flavor and the
meaning a little bit different. Sidney's neat jest at the end, for
example, may seem sharper and more lively when the punctuation helps to set it up and focus our attention on it.

Here is a sentence by another writer that we can practice on.
I give it as the author wished it to appear:

Francine which is a name of a young woman who has
changed very much in five years hoped to be married that
is not hoped but attended to the waiting which was not
intentional she was very well occupied.

This is a form that it might take in performance:

Francine (which is a name of a young woman who has
changed very much in five years) hoped to be married—
that is, not hoped but attended to the waiting, which was
not intentional. She was very well occupied.

This performance will doubtless seem faintly unsatisfactory, as
if we didn't quite understand the sentence and therefore couldn't
read it adequately. And perhaps this is the case. It is from Ger-
trude Stein's *How To Write* (1931), in the conservation chapter
called "Saving the Sentence." The problem (or our problem, at
least) seems to lie in dealing with the logical relations between
the several components of the sentence while trying to save this
particular sentence. In "not hoped but attended to the waiting,"
for example, the two alternatives offered are not within our usual

pattern of dialectics. How do we deal with them? Punctuation does not tidy up an unfamiliar pattern of logic. We have a choice of thinking up a new interpretation or condemning the passage or revising our logic or discovering some other alternative that may bring us peace.

Another writer, another style. Here is a small part of a very long passage that the author chose to present in the following fashion. It is about a personal God who

> loves us dearly with some exceptions for reasons unknown but time will tell are plunged in torment plunged in fire whose fire flames if that continues and who can doubt it will fire the firmament that is to say blast hell to heaven so blue still and calm so calm with a calm which even though intermittent is better than nothing but not so fast

Here is one way to perform this passage:

> A personal God . . . loves us dearly (with some exceptions) for reasons unknown (but time will tell) are plunged in torment, plunged in fire, whose fire flames if that continues. And who can doubt it will fire the firmament! That is to say, blast hell to heaven, so blue, still, and calm—so calm, with a calm which even though intermittent is better than nothing. But not so fast!

Not so fast indeed! Where are we? What are we talking about? What is going on? This example is a reminder of the limit of the function of signs. Punctuation cannot translate a non-logical form of expression into ordinary speech. The internal structure of prose has its own elastic strength that resists efforts to change its basic shape. This example is also a reminder of the importance of context and situation in reading a text. The passage comes from Lucky's speech near the end of the first act of Samuel Beckett's *Waiting for Godot* (1954), where it has a special function in its own terms, where much is being talked about and much is going on.

These examples are all drawn from passages in which the author chose not to give the reader the guidance that punctuation can offer. Now let me turn the tables on a couple of writers by depunctuating passages from their writings. I'd like for us to see, from the reverse angle, the guidance the author actually succeeded in giving us, or imposing on us, through the signs of punctuation, and to consider the depunctuated passage as an alternative text, or an alternative way of understanding.

Here is one passage, after I have removed all the marks of punctuation:

> the first in time and the first in importance of the influ-
> ences upon the mind is that of nature every day the sun
> and after sunset night and her stars ever the winds blow
> ever the grass grows every day men and women convers-
> ing beholding and beholden the scholar must needs stand
> wistful and admiring before this great spectacle and he
> must settle its value in his mind what is nature to him
> there is never a beginning there is never an end to the
> inexplicable continuity of this web of God but always cir-
> cular power returning into itself

Those who do not immediately recognize the passage are probably understanding it in a way that is somewhat different from
their ordinary reading of it. Without punctuation, the passage
flows along almost irresistibly, pushing all before it, mingling
specifics and abstractions, integrating nature and man and God
into one timeless pattern.

The passage comes from the beginning of the first section of
Emerson's "The American Scholar." Here is the way that Emerson actually presented it:

> The first in time and the first in importance of the influ-
> ences upon the mind is that of nature. Every day, the sun;
> and, after sunset, night and her stars. Ever the winds
> blow; ever the grass grows. Every day, men and women,
> conversing, beholding and beholden. The scholar must
> needs stand wistful and admiring before this great spec-
> tacle. He must settle its value in his mind. What is nature
> to him? There is never a beginning, there is never an end
> to the inexplicable continuity of this web of God, but al-
> ways circular power returning into itself.

What is changed by depunctuating the passage? People might
give different answers. I think: first of all, some inconvenience
to the reader, but not much. The relation of one thought to what
follows it is within the pattern of logic that we are accustomed

to dealing with, and we can adjust without too much difficulty
to the unconventional presentation. The reader has to be willing
to move along at about half speed through the passage, to be
sure. Without punctuation, there is more of a sense of dramatic
impetuosity; with punctuation, more of a sense of logical dis-
crimination, maybe even a touch of fussiness.

Emerson's prose has been much praised (touted, perhaps) in
recent years for its relation to what has come to be called "poet's
prose." Here is another example which I have depunctuated:

> thou shalt have the whole land for thy park and manor
> the sea for thy bath and navigation without tax and with-
> out envy the woods and the rivers thou shalt own and
> thou shalt possess that wherein others are only tenants
> and boarders thou true land-lord sea-lord air-lord wher-
> ever snow falls or water flows or birds fly wherever day
> and night meet in twilight wherever the blue heaven is
> hung by clouds or sown with stars wherever are forms
> with transparent boundaries wherever are outlets into ce-
> lestial space wherever is danger and awe and love there is
> beauty plenteous as rain shed for thee and though thou
> shouldest walk the world over thou shalt not be able to
> find a condition inopportune or ignoble

These are the concluding lines of "The Poet." Here is the way
that Emerson in fact chose to present this conclusion to his peroration:

> Thou shalt have the whole land for thy park and manor,
> the sea for thy bath and navigation, without tax and with-
> out envy; the woods and the rivers thou shalt own; and
> thou shalt possess that wherein others are only tenants
> and boarders. Thou true land-lord! sea-lord! air-lord!
> Wherever snow falls, or water flows, or birds fly, wherever
> day and night meet in twilight, wherever the blue heaven
> is hung by clouds, or sown with stars, wherever are forms
> with transparent boundaries, wherever are outlets into
> celestial space, wherever is danger, and awe, and love,
> there is Beauty, plenteous as rain, shed for thee, and
> though thou shouldest walk the world over, thou shalt not
> be able to find a condition inopportune or ignoble.

It seems to me, again, that not very much logical sense was lost by depunctuation, but the meaning has been changed by the decided alteration of tone. The depunctuated passage bespeaks meditation, the original conveys enthusiasm.

Both of the two essays by Emerson from which I have quoted passages were written for delivery as addresses (or orations, even) by a man who was a notably skillful speaker. Good oratory tends to be self-interpreting through its amenability to performance, and the guidance of punctuation may be less needed. Moreover, the elevated, prophetic strain manages pretty well on its own, and may even increase in the intensity of its oracular power when loosed from the bonds of punctuation. Some variety or other of the prophetic strain is strong in a good many nineteenth- and twentieth-century writers who have sometimes minimized punctuation, like Mallarmé, Whitman, Apollinaire, William Carlos Williams, and John Ashbery. It may be that a subconscious recognition of the power of the prophetic strain encouraged them to free themselves from the conventions of punctuation.

A different kind of strain and a different kind of need is often evident in critical writings. Here is a short passage of two sentences, from an essay in literary criticism, that I have taken the liberty of depunctuating:

> anything that relieves responsible prose of the duty of being while placed before us good enough interesting enough and if the question be of picture pictorial enough above all in itself does it the worst of services and may well inspire in the lover of literature certain lively questions as to the future of that institution that one should as an author reduce one's reader artistically inclined to such a state of hallucination by the images one has evoked as doesn't permit him to rest till he has noted or recorded them set up some semblance of them in his own other art nothing could better consort than that I naturally allow with the desire or the pretension to cast a literary spell

I think that this famous passage deserves careful study in its depunctuated as well as in its original form. It may not be easy to come to terms with, and might profit from a second view. It has a special interest for us because it embodies a lot of features characteristic of a main stream of critical writing of the last fifty years or so. If it were described as being a generation or two in the past, might we say that it has a flavor of Kenneth Burke or R. P. Blackmur? If it were said to be of the more recent past, might we say that it has an affinity to some writings of Paul de Man or Michael Riffaterre?

Perhaps so but no. It is, of course, a lesson of the master, Henry James. Here is the passage in the way that he presented it, in the Preface to the New York Edition of *The Golden Bowl* (1916):

> Anything that relieves responsible prose of the duty of being, while placed before us, good enough, interesting enough, and, if the question be of picture, pictorial enough, above all *in itself*, does it the worst of services, and may well inspire in the lover of literature certain lively questions as to the future of that institution. That one should, as an author, reduce one's reader, 'artistically' inclined, to such a state of hallucination by the images one has evoked as doesn't permit him to rest till he has noted or recorded them, set up some semblance of them in his own other medium, by his own other art—nothing could better consort than *that*, I naturally allow, with the desire or the pretension to cast a literary spell.

What are we to think of the James passage without punctuation? I think: that it is difficult (perhaps obscure) because the main drift of the thought can be readily confused with the secondary issues or with the qualifications that circle around, looking for a place to come to rest. In the meantime, we must hold the entire verbal construct and all that it stands for in a state of suspense, while it floats around up there above our heads. Readers of German have perhaps better training at this expedient.

James's manner incorporates secondary issues and qualifications into the main drift in the hope (I suppose) of a more accurate and precise communication. The structure of English allows this tactic only to a limited degree before confusion sets in. Henry James sometimes carried this tactic into the borderlands of confusion, and so have some literary critics of the last generation, while striving (in James's manner) for a degree of nuance that English does not embrace without putting up at least a quiet struggle against this form of seduction.

With this kind of structure, the reader needs all the help he can get in order to be able to interpret the text adequately. In such cases, punctuation is a useful aid, sometimes even essentially a part of the text.

Through these several examples, I have been trying to suggest something of the ways that punctuation works as a guide to understanding. It has a potentially important role, but the range of its value is wide—sometimes it does only a little, sometimes a lot. But it does more, perhaps, than we generally realize in guiding the way we understand and in setting the tone. Most of all, it has an important bearing on how we perform the text.

Popular songwriters have a keen awareness of the interpretive power of punctuation. The way in which their lyrics are punctuated may (they feel) suggest a kind of performance that will be out of step with the music. Ira Gershwin (who is perhaps the most distinguished American writer of such lyrics) has explained how some songwriters take special pains to avoid conflict between words and music by given precedence to music. In his charming *Lyrics on Several Occasions* (1959, pp. 299–302), he tells how songwriters demonstrate a new song to a publisher or to some possible performer. They give the publisher or the performer a copy of the text, all in capital letters, and without any punctuation at all. Thus the music—and not the punctuation or the typography—provides the primary key for where the emphases shall fall and where the pauses shall occur.

The theory of the text that this book develops—and on which it is built—is that the realization of any text is its performance. On this principle, any text becomes usable through reading it, whether that reading is aloud or silent. Every reading, in turn, constitutes a new performance (and a new interpretation, or understanding) of the text. Everything I shall have to say about reading English prose has a relation to this idea.

The most useful simple analogy to reading—which is (I repeat once more) the performance of a text—is that of a musician playing a score. The playing is a performance; the musician realizes the score as a reader realizes a text. The realization may take an unlimited variety of forms. It may be expert or crude or appealing or blundering or polished or whatever, and every performance may (or may not) differ from every other one in large or small ways. But this is the character of the performance, whether playing or reading.

The score (or the text) is as it was before, available for any other performance that may be attempted, unchanged by this performance. The performance has an impact not on the score or on the text but on the performer and on any who have witnessed that performance or who have been otherwise influenced by it, directly or indirectly. If we later carry around with us, inside ourselves, a memory of the occasion, it is usually a memory of the performance. We may also carry around a memory of the text as a series of signs. But that memory is without life until we perform the text.

2.

CONVENTION AND PERFORMANCE
The Development of Punctuation

From the time we are young, we are taught how to do a great many routine and mechanical things in accordance with rules. Punctuation is one of them. We are sometimes given to understand that the rules that govern punctuation are among the eternal verities. That a comma before a non-restrictive clause is a logical necessity to prevent the return of chaos and old night. That one between principal clauses joined by a coordinating conjunction is a finger in the dyke against illiteracy.

In lay language about writing, "style" is taken to mean, essentially, the proper attention to these and similar details. And books with *Style* in the title tend to be manuals of instruction on such matters. Occasionally they are witty and urbane (like Strunk and White), but mostly they try to appeal to the child within us who would like to please the grown-ups. This kind of Style is monitored by experts who do indeed know when a form of address should be capitalized and when a number should be written out but who cannot necessarily compose a good English sentence.

These matters of style, on which so much weight is frequently laid, are all conventions. The *MLA Style Sheet* and the *Chicago Manual of Style* and other handbooks sanctify conventions and make them seem forever. Such books do lengthen the life of the conventions. But they are still conventions, and they still change very greatly over a period of time.

There are some hard questions that can be asked about the conventions of punctuation. Like these. What are the major changes that have taken place in punctuation from the late Middle Ages to our times? Why have the conventions changed? What are the needs that lead to new conventions? What effects do these conventions have on the structure of English prose? Or on our reading (or performance or understanding) of the text? If a text uses a set of conventions that are not our own, is our reading of that text different from the reading of persons who accepted (or accept) those particular conventions?

I would like to offer a few examples that give hints about the ways that the conventions of punctuation have been changing since the time of the introduction of printing. As we move along, I will try to suggest possible answers to some of the questions I have raised. Although they are all related in one way or another, those of particular importance to us are the questions about the effects of the conventions on how we read prose and how we perform texts.

I

But first, a little background on the earlier conventions of punctuation. That history is complex and to some degree uncertain, but a rough outline can be offered of the main line of development, in Greek and Roman and medieval sources, with the understanding that exceptions and even important details will have to be passed over. And that there is a good deal about it that I do not thoroughly understand—nor do most others, to judge by the scholarship on the subject.

Early Greek writing was normally continuous, without division between words or sentences, until at least the 5th century B.C. for inscriptions and the 4th century B.C. for manuscripts. Thereafter, occasionally (but infrequently) words or phrases were separated by a dot or a vertical line of two or three dots. The only punctuation mentioned by Aristotle was the *paragraphos,* which was a hyphen placed below the first word of a line, to indicate that the sense was going to reach a conclusion somewhere within that line. About the beginning of the 2nd century B.C., Aristophanes of Byzantium, the Librarian at Alexandria, offered (along with symbols to indicate quantity and accent) a system of marks for textual scholars to use in indicating where sections of different lengths ended within a text: that the end of a short section be marked by a dot (or period) in the middle of the line, that the end of a longer section be marked by a dot at the bottom of the line, and that the end of the longest section be marked by a dot at the top of the line. His system never really caught on, but scribes began to use dots to indicate some sort of break in the text. In Greek rhetoric, a scheme of *colometry* was devised to divide texts into word-groups in order to facilitate public reading of the texts. In this uncertain fashion, "punctuation" moved from the modest job of indicating separation between words or phrases on to the role of dividing a discourse into parts.

In Roman inscriptions, words were generally separated by dots or points, but in early Latin manuscripts after the 2d century A.D. the text was written continuously. (In earlier Latin books and codices, there had been occasional separations between words by a dot or with a gap or a dot at the end of the sentence, but this practice seems to have been abandoned.) A new topic was sometimes indicated by projecting the first letters of the initial word into the left margin.

In the early medieval period, words began to be generally separated, though it was not until about the 13th century that prepositions were finally divided from the words that followed them. The end of a sentence was indicated by a space and often by two or three dots. Gradually the use of dots at different heights to indicate different kinds of pauses was given up, and a new series of signs—the predecessors of our modern marks, though with different names and different uses—was developed from a system of musical notation. The virgule (or slash mark) came into use, sometimes to indicate a break like our period, and sometimes as an indication of a light stop, like our comma, which seems to have been derived from it. Grammarians of the early Christian era and of the Middle Ages used three kinds of punctuation marks, and they used them primarily as signs for breathing pauses.

In the Middle Ages, punctuation was used mainly to serve the needs of oral reading and declamation—to indicate where to pause for breath, and for how long. Since reading was essentially an oral discourse, the exigencies of breathing required first attention. It was only secondarily that punctuation was seen as an aid to clarifying the sense of a passage; for that purpose, punctuation was intended to aid interpretation of the deeper meaning of a text if the elements might otherwise be subject to confusion. These practices and priorities continued to be controlling through the Middle Ages and even through the 16th century. In fact, a residue of this use of punctuation continued, as we shall see, at least through the middle of the 19th century. (Walter J. Ong has provided extensive details on theories of punctuation in his valuable essay on "Historical Backgrounds of

Elizabethan and Jacobean Punctuation Theory," *PMLA*, 59 (1944), 349–60.)

Since punctuation was so closely related to reading aloud, it is worth reviewing—very briefly—the ways in which reading has changed in the last millenium. We generally assume that the normal way to read is silently. People who move their lips or sound out the words are thought of as beginners or incompetent readers. And perhaps this is true for us, but it is not a general truth.

In the last fifty years, a number of studies have emphasized the importance and the power of the oral as opposed to the written mode of communication. Here are some of the conclusions. That early society was ordered and governed by oral tradition. That early epic poems were composed and transmitted orally. That the commonest method of "writing" through the Middle Ages was by oral dictation to a scribe. That vernacular literary works were often explicitly addressed, in the Middle Ages, to an audience of hearers rather than of readers. That habitual memorization (rather than writing things down) was common practice and a habit of mind until the 12th or 13th centuries, and that it persisted even after that time. That reliance on written records (as opposed to human memory) came to be important about that same time, when records proliferated and set the stage for a great increase in literacy. That there was an early preference for reading aloud, and that this preference continued throughout the Middle Ages, and beyond. That modern scholars have tended to be prejudiced in favor of literacy (as opposed to oral expression) as a civilizing force. M. T. Clanchy has provided a summary of past work along these lines, as well as his own contributions to the subject, in *From Memory to Written Record* (Cambridge: Harvard University Press, 1979).

The shift from oral reading (the early practice) to silent reading (our practice) began to take place (so far as the European experience is concerned) within the monasteries. Until the 12th century, monastic reading (or reading the text, aloud, as a way of using the text in spiritual exercises) had been dominant. This form of reading then began to take second place in monasteries to scholastic reading (or study of the text, often or usually silently, for its learning). Reading aloud continued to be common for several centuries, however, some for groups or family gatherings, but also for the benefit of the reader himself in trying to understand the text thoroughly.

Later examples of the practice abound. It was a common Victorian family custom, the evening at home with the newest part of a novel, for example. It has frequently provided a focus for combined social and intellectual activity. And it continues to be a normal part of the educational process in school classrooms today. These examples are only a modest reminder, however, of the persistent tradition of what was long the main form of reading.

Reading aloud is explicit performance of the text. It is my impression that this way of dealing with a text of literary expectations has been very much more common throughout our history—including the modern period—than scholars and critics have assumed. Indeed, this kind of performance has been generally ignored, at least so far as its bearing on the text is concerned, even by critics who center their work on reading as creative experience.

If we forget the tradition of reading aloud, we run many risks in dealing with texts of earlier times. In our silent reading, we may tend to ignore the whole sense of performance, which was an implicit part of the text during the times in question. Or, we assume that our way of reading is the "right" way to respond to the text—when in fact our way may distort the text. Anachronism is just as possible in our assumptions about how a text was read as it is in our attribution of the current meaning to a word (like "prevent") when that word had an entirely different signification at the time of the text.

II

Now to go on with a sketch of the modern development of punctuation. An important change took place along with the introduction into Europe of printing from moveable type, in the latter 15th century. Printers tended to follow scribal manuscript practice in punctuation as they did for nearly everything else. There was a corrector of the press as there had been a corrector of manuscripts in the scriptorium. Punctuation was thought in general to be the responsibility of the printer, as it had been of the scribe or corrector before him. But there were changes in punctuation, and those changes are significant.

Here is an early example of what happened to punctuation in the printing office. First, a short passage from the only early extant manuscript of the writings of Sir Thomas Malory, called the Winchester Manuscript, written down about 1485. (In this transcript, I have modernized only the spelling.) It is the beginning of "The Tournament at Surluse," featuring Sir Galahad:

> So it befell that Galahad the high prince lord of the country of Surluse whereof came out many good knights and this noble prince was a passing good man of arms and ever he held a noble fellowship together and then he came to King Arthurs court and told him his intent how this was his will he had let cry a joust in the country of Surluse the which country was within the bounds of King Arthur and there he asked leave to cry a joust I will give you leave said King Arthur But wyte you well I may not be there myself // Sir said Queen Guinevere please it you to give me leave to be at that joust with right a good will said King Arthur for Sir Galahad the good prince shall have you in governance

The only mark of punctuation in the passage is that double virgule or slash mark, equal perhaps to our period or full stop. But we must imagine that when this passage was read—aloud—it was read with pauses and emphases and all the rest to convey a clear understanding of the text. The skill of readers was apparently such that they could perform the text effectively without the guidance of punctuation.

Now let me offer the same passage in the form in which it first appeared in print. That was in the noble book printed by William Caxton in 1485, approximately the same date as the only early manuscript; Caxton entitled his book *Le Morte d'Arthur*, thus fixing forever an inappropriate title on this great cycle of Arthurian romances. He was working from a manuscript that is now lost, but the wording of this passage is almost identical with that of the Winchester Manuscript. I have modernized the spelling and the type but retained Caxton's punctuation, here limited to the virgule, the equivalent sometimes of our comma, sometimes of our period.

So it befell that Sir Galahad the high prince was lord of

the country of Surluse / whereof came many good knights / And this noble prince was a passing good man of arms and ever he held a noble fellowship together / And then he came to Arthurs court / and told him his intent / how this was his will / how he would let cry a joust in the country of Surluse / the which country was within the lands of King Arthur / and there he asked leave to let cry a joust / I will give you leave said King Arthur / But wyte thou well said King Arthur / I may not be there / Sir said Queen Guinevere please it you to give me leave to be at that joust / with right good will said Arthur / for Sir Galahad the high prince shall have you in governance /

The punctuation of this passage in the manuscript was limited to one double virgule (or full stop) at the end of a major part of the discourse and at a change of speakers. Caxton uses fifteen virgules; they come after natural groups of words, and they seem to be intended as signs for where to pause for breath in reading the passage aloud. There could be more pauses indicated—after "high prince" and "man of arms," for example. Or there could be fewer, without serious harm or change of principle.

We would punctuate the passage on quite a different theory from that of indicating pauses for breathing, and our theory would give us less latitude in the specific details. Here is a way that we might punctuate it:

So it befell that Sir Galahad, the high prince, was lord of the country of Surluse, whereof came many good knights. And this noble prince was a passing good man of arms, and ever he held a noble fellowship together. And then he came to Arthur's court and told him his intent, how this was his will: how he would let cry a joust in the country of Surluse, the which country was within the lands of King Arthur. And there he asked leave to let cry a joust.

"I will give you leave," said King Arthur. "But wyte you well," said King Arthur, "I may not be there."

"Sir," said Queen Guinevere, "please it you to give me leave to be at that joust?"

"With right good will," said Arthur, "for Sir Galahad, the high prince, shall have you in governance."

If Caxton's punctuation looks odd to us, we can imagine that ours would look equally odd to him.

> *Caxton*: wherefore befell it that this my pleasant book has been so bruised and broken with such a power of signs like unto necromancy laid upon it the which serve no purpose for those who know to read

> *You*: This is our style of punctuation. We use it to guide the reader to an easier and clearer understanding of the construction of the sentences and hence of the text as a whole.

> *Caxton*: then believe you not in the power of the text that runs of its own strength and virtue into the minds and remembrancing of those who do exercise their wits after it

> *You*: Perhaps not. We have come to rely on these aids to faster reading, and we feel puzzled or lost without them.

Another brief example of Caxton's practice, this time from his beginning of "The Noble Tale of Sir Lancelot of the Lake," may help to clarify the practice of using punctuation to indicate breathing pauses:

> Soon after that King Arthur was come / from Rome into England / then all the knights of the table round resorted unto the king / and made many jousts and tournaments /

Notice that the virgules are at what seem to be natural breathing pauses. It happens, as it almost always does, that the groups of words within the breathing pauses also combine to make units of sense. But the breathing pauses are paramount.

In comparison with the practice that lay behind them, the early printers were much more lavish with punctuation than the scribes had been. The reasons for this radical increase are not hard to seek. The ability to read was a relatively rare and developed accomplishment before the advent of the printed book. The printed book brought texts to a much wider audience, and the widening of the audience had to include many who were less experienced and less expert in reading, and many who were learners. The additional punctuation was presumably for the guidance of those readers as to where to pause. And—a matter which the early printers had much in mind—the additional punctuation would, by contributing to the convenience of those readers, presumably increase the sales of their books.

Here are a couple of small examples from the middle of the 16th century, about a century after the beginning of printing. The virgules have disappeared and familiar marks have taken their place. This is from the first English translation of Sir Thomas More's *Utopia,* printed in London in 1551, with the spelling modernized. The dedicatory epistle begins in this fashion:

> Upon a time, when tidings came to the city of Corinth that King Philip father to Alexander surnamed the Great, was coming thitherward with an army royal to lay siege to the city. The Corinthians being forthwith stricken with great fear, began busily, and earnestly to look about them, and to fall to work of all hands.

And here is the opening of the Second Book:

> The island of Utopia, containeth in breadth in the middle part of it (for there it is broadest) 200 miles. Which breadth continueth through the most part of the land. Saving that by little and little it cometh in, and waxeth narrower towards both the ends. Which fetching about a circuit or compass of 500 miles, do fashion the whole island like to the new moon.

The punctuation marks are familiar, but the way they are used is not. They break the discourse into smaller units, and they suggest places to pause for breath. But they have little regard for indicating where the sentences end or what the relations are between subordinate clauses and main clauses.

> Mr. Gradgrind: You say not nearly enough, Sir. This foul practice wickedly separates the subject from its very own verb, and it undertakes to pass off subordinate clauses as if they were proper and complete sentences. The perpetrators of this nonsense should be soundly whipped. That should bring them to their senses and prevent the spread of this illiteracy amongst simple and ignorant folk.

The Mr. Gradgrind within us would like to impose our conventions on everybody, past, present, and future. If we follow his doctrine, we will understand everything, to be sure, but we will understand it all as an image of ourselves.

III

We noticed that Caxton ventured to add punctuation to the text of *Le Morte d'Arthur.* Before going on to consider the ways that the conventions of punctuation developed in later centuries, it is worth pausing briefly to consider who, in the past, was generally responsible for punctuating English prose. And who established the theories and principles of punctuation that were followed.

In the early centuries of printing, it was the printers who generally felt themselves responsible for the "accidentals" of the text—for the punctuation, the spelling, the capitalization, and the italicization. The kind of contribution that Caxton made to the punctuation of texts was repeated over and over again in the process of book production from the time of the beginning of printing pretty much through the 19th century, at least. Sometimes more, sometimes less. I use the term "printer" as shorthand. In the beginning, it was literally the printer who was responsible for the punctuation. As the production and distribution of books changed over the centuries, the precise location of the editorial function shifted, in the change from printer to bookseller to publisher, but always within the editorial and production (rather than the authorial) side of bookmaking.

From the earliest times, both writers and printers accepted this state of affairs. Most writers (like Gray, Wordsworth, Byron, James Fenimore Cooper, Charlotte Brontë, and Yeats) were delighted to have someone else do the punctuating for them. In the 20th century, writers tended more toward taking care of their own punctuation, and a few (like A. E. Housman and Max Beerbohm) insisted on it as a matter of high principle. More recently, punctuation has come to be thought of as the task of the writer, but editors still feel free to clean up punctuation that doesn't follow their house rules.

To discharge their responsibility, early printers developed handbooks of style and began to standardize the marks of punctuation. In 1566, the scholarly Aldine Press in Venice published a treatise that formalized a system of punctuation to indicate four degrees of pauses. In England, Joseph Moxon's *Mechanick Exer-*

cises on the Whole Art of Printing (1683) was the first of the many important English and American printers' manuals to appear. These manuals exhort compositors and proofreaders to supply or correct the punctuation of their copy in accordance with current practice. A full treatment of the ways that writers and printers have shared the responsibility for dealing with accidentals from the 16th to the 20th centuries is contained in my *Principles of Textual Criticism* (Huntington Library, 1972), pp. 131–70.

Printers generally took care of the practice of punctuating the text, but the theories under which they worked were developed and expounded by rhetoricians and grammarians. These learned persons produced thousands of treatises, which have guided and influenced writers, printers, and the preparers of school texts. I have mentioned Walter J. Ong's valuable resumé of the purport of these treatises from early Christian times (Donatus, of the 4th century, for the prime example) to the 16th century (including such as Ramus 1572, Mulcaster 1582, and Puttenham 1589) ("Historical Backgrounds of Elizabethan and Jacobean Punctuation Theory," *PMLA*, 59, 1944, 349–60). The primary role of punctuation was seen as an indication of pauses for breathing, as a guide to oral reading. Gradually, the writers of these treatises began to view punctuation, in addition, as an aid toward understanding the sense of the passage in the text.

The number of these treatises greatly increased in the next three centuries. A sampling of the most important and influential and frequently reprinted writers might include Butler (1634), Daines (1640), Brightland (1711), Robertson (1785), and Wilson (1844). At the beginning of the 17th century, punctuation theory continued the earlier idea that it was to show where to pause for breath. At the same time, a theory was set forth with increasing insistence that punctuation should clarify not only the sense of the passage but also the grammatical structure of the sentence. The theories were vague and perhaps contradictory, but they were asserted with confidence. The need was felt (especially by printers) for specific rules about punctuation. By the middle of the 19th century, this need was filled by treatises which set forth detailed and precise rules and also established the grammatical structure of the sentence (or the syntax) as the basis for punctuation. This basis has continued (with contrary practice by a relatively few dissidents) as the standard theory and practice into our own time. A valuable discussion of some representative treatises is contained in Park Honan's "Eighteenth and Nineteenth Century English Punctuation Theory," *English Studies,* 41 (1960), 92–102.

In our own time, many scholarly editors of works of the past have taken the liberty of fixing the punctuation in accordance with modern usage, of "modernizing" the punctuation in order to make the text more accessible to the modern reader. On the other hand, some editors may have shared Samuel Johnson's sentiments in his Preface to Shakespeare: "I have considered the punctuation as wholly in my power; for what could be their care of colons and commas, who corrupted words and sentences. Whatever could be done by adjusting points is therefore silently performed, in some plays with much diligence, in others with less; it is hard to keep a busy eye steadily fixed upon evanescent atoms, or a discursive mind upon evanescent truth."

This cavalier attitude is far from true of the editors of the great modern scholarly editions, whose scrupulosity makes punctuation at times seem the central mystery of our textual faith. But the makers of lesser editions and of textbooks and of anthologies ordinarily do not share this faith. The passages in the following section are intentionally familiar and readily available. But I soon discovered that I could not count on the handy modern sources of these texts if I wanted to reproduce the original punctuation and that I had, in prudence, to return to an original print.

IV

For our purposes, the importance of the changes in the theory of punctuation is the effect that they have on the structure of English prose, and the way we read it. We have looked at a couple of examples from the late 15th and mid-16th centuries. A few later examples may serve to clarify the issues.

Here is the beginning of Francis Bacon's essay entitled "Of Honor and Reputation" (with the spelling modernized) as it appeared in his first collection in 1597:

> The winning of honor is but the revealing of a mans virtue and worth without disadvantage, for some in their actions do affect honor and reputation, which sort of men

are commonly much talked of, but inwardly little admired: and some darken their virtue in the show of it, so as they be undervalued in opinion.

Here is the same passage (with the spelling modernized) as it appeared in the 1625 edition. This is the last (and much enlarged) version of his essays that Bacon prepared, but the punctuation was (as usual) doubtless the work of the printer:

The winning of honor, is but the revealing of a mans virtue and worth, without disadvantage. For some in their actions, do woo and affect honor, and reputation: Which sort of men, are commonly much talked of, but inwardly little admired. And some, contrariwise, darken their virtue, in the show of it; So as they be undervalued in opinion.

It is interesting to notice the wide variation in the punctuation of the two versions. In the 1597 version there are four commas, one colon, and one period; the word groups are relatively long and uniform in size. In 1625, there are nine commas, one semicolon, one colon, and three periods. The heavier punctuation of 1625 slows the movement of the discourse by breaking it down into more than twice as many breathing passages. The slowness of the movement could be made to create a stately or serious effect. It is the same kind of punctuation that we saw in the print of the *Utopia*; it does not clarify the syntax, and it is equally subject to Mr. Gradgrind's objections. But it does give us some hints about the ways that Bacon's essays were read by his contemporaries.

When we move to the writings of Ben Jonson, we come to one who has the name for having been the most particular writer of his time on the theory and practice of punctuation. He had read the standard authorities (notably Ramus and Mulcaster), and he devoted a chapter to his *English Grammar* (published posthumously, in 1640) to the four "distinctions" of punctuation, the period, colon, comma, and semi-colon. All of these marks were intended to help the breathing "when we pronounce any *Sentence*," as well as for grammatical purposes; they are "as well for the speakers ease, as for the plainer deliverance of the things spoken." For Jonson, a "perfect sentence" ends with a period or (if joined to another "perfect sentence") with a colon; an "imperfect sentence" uses a comma or a semi-colon, depending on the length of the breathing.

Jonson's earlier published writings, such as the quartos of his plays, were lightly punctuated. By the time of the publication of his folio in 1616—the first collected edition of the "Works" of any English writer—he had developed the more systematic method of punctuation that he set forth in his *English Grammar*; he himself added punctuation in the folio (even in the proofs) and made it heavier. Here is a small sample from the folio, the beginning of Jonson's dedication of *Catiline* to the Earl of Pembroke. (I have modernized the spelling.)

> In so thick, and dark an ignorance, as now almost covers the age, I crave leave to stand near your light: and, by that, to be read. Posterity may pay your benefit the honor, & thanks: when it shall know, that you dare, in these jig-given times, to countenance a legitimate poem.

Care for punctuation he had. Concern for the guidance of the reader through his syntax he had not. The punctuation does offer guidance to a way of pausing in the course of reading in order to create a dramatic effect. The pauses for the colons, for example, set apart and emphasize what is to follow—they turn out to be words about Jonson himself: his wish to be read, and his literary achievement.

Change in conventions sometimes comes very slowly. The change in punctuation is relatively minor in the century and a half between the English *Utopia* and Dryden's last works. Here is the opening of Dryden's last major essay, his Preface to the *Fables*, written and published in the year of his death, 1700. (I present this and all following passages *without* modernization.)

> 'Tis with a Poet, as with a Man who designs to build, and is very exact, as he supposes, in casting up the Cost beforehand: But, generally speaking, he is mistaken in his Account, and reckons short of the Expence he first intended: He alters his Mind as the Work proceeds, and will have this or that Convenience more, of which he had not thought when he began. So has it hapned to me; I have built a House, where I intended but a Lodge: Yet

with better Success than a certain Nobleman, who beginning with a Dog-kennil, never liv'd to finish the Palace he
had contriv'd.

As in the *Utopia,* this passage has rather heavy punctuation:
twelve commas, one semi-colon, three colons, and two periods.
The punctuation is doing the same kind of work that we have
noticed in earlier passages. Here it creates a kind of ruminative
effect. There are many great pauses and lesser pauses and looking backward over the shoulder, as if there were uncertainty
about what might be lurking around the corner. All the colons
are marking the ends of "perfect" sentences, and the intimation
therefore is that the idea of the preceding sentence is joined with
the sense of the one that follows it. This style gives a sense of
continuousness, or a feeling that the totality of the meaning is
being suspended all the way through the passage, and that you
have not concluded until you have concluded.

It was a little of a surprise to me to realize that Addison's
manner of punctuation is quite similar to Dryden's, though the
effect is different. Here is a small passage from Addison, the
beginning of Number 122 of *The Spectator* for Friday, 20 July
1711:

> A Man's first Care should be to avoid the Reproaches of
> his own Heart; his next, to escape the Censures of the
> World: If the last interferes with the former, it ought to
> be entirely neglected; but otherwise, there cannot be a
> greater Satisfaction to an honest Mind, than to see those
> Approbations which it gives itself seconded by the Ap-
> plauses of the Publick: A Man is more sure of his Con-
> duct, when the Verdict which he passes upon his own
> Behaviour is thus warranted, and confirmed by the Opin-
> ion of all that know him.

There are as many strong breaks indicated here as for the only
slightly longer passage from Dryden. The semi-colons and the
colons are used as Dryden used them, to mark long breathing
pauses and slow down the movement. Here they set a sedate pace
for the progress of the passage. The impact of the condensed
and aphoristic beginning is strengthened by the use of the
breathing spaces to draw out its effect.

For Samuel Johnson, the opening of his Preface to Shakespeare (1765) is an interesting example of the guidance that punctuation offers.

> That praises are without reason lavished on the dead, and that the honours due only to excellence are paid to antiquity, is a complaint likely to be always continued by those, who, being able to add nothing to truth, hope for eminence from the heresies of paradox; or those, who, being forced by disappointment upon consolatory expedients, are willing to hope from posterity what the present age refuses, and flatter themselves that the regard which is yet denied by envy, will be at last bestowed by time.

This passage (of approximately the same length as the two preceding ones) has about the same amount of punctuation that they do. But here the marks are almost all commas (with one semi-colon to signal a change in direction), and they mainly suggest the places to make brief pauses for breath throughout the passage without losing heart on the way. The placement of the last comma is typical: "the regard which is yet denied by envy, will be at last bestowed by time"; the comma serves the purpose of providing one last place to pause for strength for a triumphant arrival at the end of this long sentence. The punctuation helps the reader make his way through a sentence that is relatively straightforward but relatively breathtaking.

Wordsworth's Preface to the *Lyrical Ballads* of 1800 is justly celebrated for its place in the history of literary criticism. Here are the first two paragraphs of it, in the form in which they first appeared:

> The First Volume of these Poems has already been submitted to general perusal. It was published, as an experiment which, I hoped, might be of some use to ascertain, how far, by fitting to metrical arrangement a selection of the real language of men in a state of vivid sensation, that sort of pleasure and that quantity of pleasure may be imparted, which a Poet may rationally endeavour to impart.
>
> I had formed no very inaccurate estimate of the probable effect of those Poems: I flattered myself that they

who should be pleased with them would read them with more than common pleasure: and on the other hand I was well aware that by those who should dislike them they would be read with more than common dislike. The result has differed from my expectation in this only, that I have pleased a greater number, than I ventured to hope I should please.

In comparison with the three preceding passages (from Dryden, Addison, and Johnson), these two paragraphs are more lightly punctuated. In the first paragraph, the punctuation is mostly interventive, breaking the sense into relatively small units; it provides frequent pauses for breath without necessary regard for the grammatical structure. It conveys a sense of hesitancy, even uncertainty, about what is being said. The pauses in the second paragraph are less frequent but more decided. The colon is used in the same manner that we have observed it in every example quoted in this section—to indicate a long breathing pause between complete but related sentences. The sense of hesitancy of the first paragraph gives way, through the punctuation as well as the language, to a feeling of firmness and decisiveness.

From Wordsworth, we move on through the 19th century to Matthew Arnold. This short passage is from *Culture and Anarchy* (1869), part of the first chapter, later known under the title of "Sweetness and Light":

> The impulse of the English race towards moral development and self-conquest has nowhere so powerfully manifested itself as in Puritanism; nowhere has Puritanism found so adequate an expression as in the religious organisation of the Independents. The modern Independents have a newspaper, the *Nonconformist,* written with great sincerity and ability. The motto, the standard, the profession of faith which this organ of theirs carries aloft, is: "The Dissidence of Dissent and the Protestantism of the Protestant religion." There is sweetness and light, and an ideal of complete harmonious human perfection! One need not go to culture and poetry to find language to judge it.

This passage has about the same amount of punctuation as

those by Dryden, Addison, and Johnson. Unlike the earlier examples, however, here the longer stops predominate over the comma. Here there is plenty of time to pause for breath, to regroup forces, and to drive ahead with full vigor. No hesitancy is suggested by the structure here. On the contrary, it is all confidence and certainty.

Most important of all, Arnold's punctuation is entirely syntactical—it clearly indicates the grammatical structure of the sentences. It would indeed be a fussy schoolteacher who took occasion to find fault with the punctuating of this passage. Rather, it might be welcomed with a sigh of relief: "Ah, at last—here is someone who knows how to punctuate!"

The passage is a reasonably fair example of the basic type of punctuation that came to be the accepted and acceptable norm in the latter part of the nineteenth century, and continues so in our own time. This is the form of punctuation that is taught in school texts and exemplified in manuals of style. Of course there are many variations and modification to it, and fiction writers often use punctuation in a very different way in dialogue to help in suggesting patterns of speech. The conventions of syntactical punctuation are probably very helpful to those who are learning a language on an analytical basis. For the rest of us, or after we have our learner's permit, the syntax generally can take care of itself without the reinforcement of punctuation to indicate the grammatical structure.

The variations of syntactical punctuation in use during the last century or so could provide interesting material for a detailed study of some features of prose style. Since the purpose of this essay is the more general one of observing (and reflecting on) the ways that conventions of punctuation affect our reading (or performing) and understanding texts, we need not pursue this history beyond the point where syntactical punctuation became commonly established.

V

In the course of looking at these various examples of English prose, scattered over many centuries, several kinds of changes are apparent in the conventions of punctuation.

The most fundamental change, perhaps, is the shift from using little or no punctuation to using a good deal or a lot. This change helped to indicate something about the structure of the prose, and therefore to direct the reader toward an interpretation. By consequence, it emphasized the idea of performance and gave clues about a way to perform the text. Change of this kind seems to have come about after notable increases in the reading public, as after the invention of printing from moveable type or after a major increase in public education. Punctuation—or more punctuation—was contrived to offer guidance to readers, in particular to new readers. But its guidance is also restrictive, as we saw in the example of Joyce's *Ulysses* in the preceding chapter.

Another kind of change was the shift from the use of punctuation as a help in oral reading to the use of punctuation as a help in silent reading. The change from oral to silent reading was of far-reaching importance. Basically, it changed the idea of the performance of the text from the natural dramatization of spoken discourse before an audience in a public situation to the need for conscious simulation through silent discourse before the self alone in a private situation. The effort necessary for performance is often faint or perfunctory without the spur of outside auditors. There have doubtless been many reasons for this change in the course of the time in which it evolved. Silent reading is much faster, and the proliferation of texts almost forces silent reading on most people. The natural communities for oral reading mostly disappeared, and the practice of reading aloud to a group has become increasingly uncommon, despite sporadic but failing efforts to present reading on television as an attractive form of cultural activity. A good deal of the prose of today—as well as that of the past—is written for the ear as well as the eye, however, and most readers continue to give at least an elementary performance of the text in silent reading if they value the text highly.

Yet another kind of change was the shift from the use of punctuation to indicate breathing pauses to the use of punctuation to indicate the grammatical structure of the sentence. The intermediate stop for this change was the use of punctuation to help clarify the meaning of the sentence, to avoid confusion in understanding the sense. This change shares some of the same initial causes with the shift from oral to silent reading. But the culmination of the ultimate move to grammatical structure as the basis for punctuation was another consequence of the spread of public education. That was when grammarians took over from their predecessors, the rhetoricians. Grammarians established the rules, and they prepared the normative textbooks for the young.

We may reflect on the significance that these changes have for us as readers who wish to come to term with texts of the past. What are the problems that we may face? What are the errors that we may unwittingly make? Here are several hints.

We have become so habituated to syntactical punctuation that we sometimes expect all prose to be punctuated on those principles, and we accept without objection the repunctuating ("modernization") of earlier texts in accordance with syntactical theory. I believe that this habituation often distorts our reading and our performance of texts of the past.

Texts that were punctuated to indicate breathing pauses will generally be interpreted quite crudely if we take the punctuation marks in their modern, syntactical significance. The colon makes an obvious problem for us, as we have seen; but so do the other marks as well. The structure of most English prose through the 18th century—and a good deal that comes later, as well—needs to be read with the punctuation as indications of where to pause for breath and how long to do so in order to perform the text effectively.

The absence (or sparseness) of punctuation in earlier times challenged the skill of the reader, to be sure. But that absence also involved the reader's sensibilities more fully in the performance of the text. Those texts challenge our own skill as readers even more than they challenged their contemporary readers.

Texts that were written in the expectation that they would be read aloud will probably not be fully realized when the performance is in silent reading. The potentialities of English encourage and reward writing and reading in which oral performance is realized, at least in the imagination. And this is yet another challenge for us.

3.

ORDERING WORDS
The Patterns of the Sentence

Mr. Walter Shandy argued powerfully in favor of auxiliary verbs as guides to a northwest passage to the intellectual world. By the right use and application of auxiliary verbs, an almost unlimited number of sentence structures can be created. Thus a whole storehouse of conceptions and conclusions could, Mr. Shandy felt, be drawn forth from a barren brain.

> The verbs auxiliary we are concerned in here, continued my father, are, *am; was; have; had; do; did; make; made; suffer; shall; should; will; would; can; could; owe; ought; used;* or *is wont.*—And these varied with tenses, *present, past, future,* and conjugated with the verb *see,*—or with these questions added to them;—*Is it? Was it? Will it be? Would it be? May it be? Might it be?* And these again put negatively, *Is it not? Was it not? Ought it not?* Or affirmatively,—*It is; It was; It ought to be.* Or chronologically,—*Has it been always? Lately? How long ago?*—Or hypothetically,—*If it was; If it was not?* What would follow? (Sterne, *Tristram Shandy,* vol. V, ch. 43)

Corporal Trim has never seen a White Bear. Yet how many thoughts can be generated for him on the subject by the proper use of auxiliary verbs! Mr. Shandy demonstrates how Corporal Trim could discourse on the subject:

> A WHITE BEAR! Very well. Have I ever seen one? Might I ever have seen one? Am I ever to see one? Ought I ever to have seen one? Or can I ever see one?
>
> Would I had seen a white bear! (for how can I imagine it?)
>
> If I should see a white bear, what would I say? If I should never see a white bear, what then?

If I never have, can, must or shall see a white bear alive;
have I ever seen the skin of one? Did I ever see one
painted?—described? Have I never dreamed of one?

Did my father, mother, uncle, aunt, brothers or sisters,
ever see a white bear? What would they give? How would
they behave? How would the white bear have behaved? Is
he wild? Tame? Terrible? Rough? Smooth?

—Is the white bear worth seeing?—

—Is there no sin in it?—

Is it better than a BLACK ONE? (vol. V, ch. 43)

The study of linguistics has likewise taught us that the way we
say sentences (surface structure) can be created by transformational rules from the way we understand sentences (deep structure). From the deep structure of *dog, bite, man,* we can generate
(by a program of simple transformation rules) the following surface structures:

> The dog bit the man.
> Did the dog bite the man?
> The dog did not bite the man.
> Did the dog not bite the man?
> The dog DID bite the man.
> The man was bitten by the dog.
> The man was not bitten by the dog.
> Was the man bitten by the dog?
> Was the man not bitten by the dog?

With a more elaborate program of transformational rules, we
can generate a larger and larger number of surface structures,
of greater and greater complexity, enough to fill a volume full
of sentences about dogs and biting and men.

Unless we have Corporal Trim's barren brain, we don't, in
fact, need much help in creating surface structures on our own.
English sentences turn out, in practice, to fill our needs for communicating through an incredibly complex variety of structures.
It is possible to analyze the structures, to name them, to describe
them synchronically and diachronically, and to consider their
syntagmatic and their paradigmatic relationships.

My purpose in this essay is simpler. To explore some examples
out of this great variety of structures of sentences in English

prose. To admire the structural design that writers have created to serve their needs and our needs. And to meditate on how different structures work, and what effects they make on us as readers.

We tend to think of the structure of the English sentence as a matter of grammar. We know something of the mysteries of the simple and the compound sentences, the complex and the compound-complex. In time of need, we can probably make, by means of a diagram, a passable graphic display of the grammatical relationships of the parts of a sentence to one another. This is a way of thinking most useful to us when we are learning the English language for the first time through formal instruction.

But there are other ways of thinking about the structure of the sentence. I want to try to explore some of them in the course of this essay and see where they lead us. The visual structure of the sentence, for one. The performance structure of the sentence, for another. Alternate structures of a given sentence, for a third. And dialectic structures of the sentence, for a fourth.

I would like to proceed with these other ways of thinking about the structure of the sentence by offering a number of familiar single sentences for consideration. The sentences are taken from the writings of notable writers of expository prose of the 16th, 17th, 18th, 19th, and 20th centuries. I have limited the number of writers to nine, and I have used (with one exception) only first sentences of major parts of their important books. I want to avoid the impression that these are odd sentences chosen from anywhere to create a special effect. The sentences that I will offer are in fact intended, when taken together, to represent in great measure the way that English prose actually works. I have (where necessary) modernized the spelling, capitalization, and punctuation of the sentences I quote so that we can focus our attention on the structure and not be diverted by other variable matters.

I

Please read each of the following three passages through one time, carefully, even though you may recognize them immediately. This is not a test of the ability to identify but an invitation to perceive.

1. I weathered some merry snow-storms
   and spent some cheerful winter evenings
   by my fireside,
   while the snow whirled wildly without
   and even the hooting of the owl
   was hushed.

2. No man is an island
   entire of itself;
   every man is a piece of the continent,
   a part of the main;
   if a clod be washed away by the sea
   Europe is the less,
   as well as if a promontory were,
   as well as if a manor of thy friend's
   or of thine own were;
   any man's death diminishes me,
   because I am involved in mankind;
   and therefore never send to know
   for whom the bell tolls;
   it tolls for thee.

3. Suddenly,
   without giving us time to arrange our thoughts
   or prepare our phrases,
   our guest has left us;
   and his withdrawal
   without farewell or ceremony
   is in keeping with his mysterious arrival,
   long years ago,
   to take up his lodging in this country.

Each of these passages is a single sentence of good English
prose. I think that the first shock of recognition that we may
have from looking at these sentences in an unfamiliar structure
is the realization that the visual structure of the sentence strongly
affects the impact that the sentence has on us. Prose has been
written and printed in lines that extend from the left margin to
the right margin of the page, without any regard to the structure
or meaning, purely as a convention dictated by economy and
simplicity. While I am not venturing to try to tear down this

useful convention, I want to suggest that the text need not take this conventional form. And that when it takes a different form, it creates a different impact.

What kind of impact? Different in detail for each reader, doubtless. In principle, a new visual structure causes these sentences to have an impact on me—and I should think on most other readers as well—that is noticeably different from the impact made on us by those sentences in their original structure. In general, for most readers, a stronger realization of the organization of the sentence, and with that a greater lucidity, perhaps. Even more important, a greater sense of closure, and with that a greater satisfaction in having gotten to where we are.

Readers who immediately identify the sources of these sentences may see them back in their earlier structure, or be unable to read them freely in the lineation that gives them the visual structure that they have here. That would be a pity, for my purposes. Whether their sources are recognized or not is otherwise of no great moment. Anyway, the first is from Thoreau's *Walden* (1854), the first sentence of the chapter entitled "Former Inhabitants; and Winter Visitors." The second passage is a sentence (well-known, thanks to Hemingway) from the middle of Donne's XVII Meditation (*Devotions*, 1624). The third passage is the first sentence of Virginia Woolf's essay on Joseph Conrad (*The Common Reader*, 1925).

Some readers may feel that these sentences have been generically altered: that arranging them into lines converts them from prose into poetry, or at least into verse. Perhaps so, under some theories of poetry. But these are temporary rearrangements, made to call attention to visual structure.

The visual structure of prose is inherently unstable, and it can be altered at will. Here are three other examples (from among the absolutely unlimited number that could be offered) to illustrate a visual structure of the sentence:

1.   Certainly
    that man were greedy of life
    who should desire to live
    when all the world
        were at an end;
  and he must needs be very impatient

> who would repine at death
> in the society of all things
> that suffer under it.

2. Though for no other cause
      yet for this:
   that posterity may know we have not
      loosely through silence
   permitted things to pass away
      as in a dream,
   there shall be for men's information
      extant thus much
   concerning the present state of the Church of God
      established amongst us
   and their careful endeavor which would have
      upheld the same.

3. Some ludicrous Schoolmen
      have put the Case
         that if an Ass were placed
            between two bundles of hay
               which affected his senses equally
               on each side
               and tempted him
               in the very same degree,
         whether it would be possible for him
         to eat of either.

I think that the visual structure given to these (and to the three earlier) sentences encourages us to read them with deliberation. Maybe because of a suspicion that we are being tested. Maybe because of the unfamiliarity of the appearance of the text. Maybe because this kind of structure is more inviting to the eyes. Maybe for all of these reasons.

As I said about the earlier examples, this kind of visual structure seems to enhance our sense of the organization of the sentence and of its closure. In fact, bringing visual perception to bear on the sentence adds another dimension to our understanding, as it does with any intellectual matter.

And it adds an element of memorability too, I think. For example, from the passage by Virginia Woolf—a sentence that is, at her level of writing, unremarkable—the close reader may well find that some of her expressions have crept into his or her storehouse of remembrances, like "arrange our thoughts," or "prepare our phrases," or even the whole

> mysterious arrival
> long years ago,
>   to take up his lodging in this country.

And it might be the same under any circumstances in which specific expressions are highlighted, as in dialogue.

The visual structure of these last three examples makes them move smoothly into our understanding. But please notice that the strict grammarian might find exceeding fault with each of them. The first passage, which is the first sentence of Sir Thomas Browne's "To the Reader" in *Religio Medici* (1643), has two long "who" clauses that our grammarian would like to see much more closely associated with the words they modify. The second passage, the first sentence of Richard Hooker's Preface to the first four books *Of the Lawes of Ecclesiasticall Politie* (1593), offers a terrible puzzle for the person who needs to diagram it and get the clause which makes up line 3–6 in my rendering into the right relation with what comes before it and what comes after. The joke about the ass and the two bundles of hay, the first sentence of Addison's *Spectator* No. 191 for October 9, 1711, makes a problem of accounting for the clause that takes up the last two lines. When we see the sentences in a visual structure, however, these problems don't obtrude themselves. Too bad we can't always see a structure of a sentence while we are reading it.

Back to the question of the resemblance of these visual and performance structures to those of verse. Consider, for example, the passage I have just quoted from Hooker ("Though for no other cause / yet for this"). I have never heard Hooker described as a writer of "poetic prose"; but the lucidity and elegance of his prose derive (aside from his diction) from the internal organization of his sentences. That organization makes it easily possible to give them a symmetrical performance structure and thus create a resemblance to a structure of verse.

II

The visual structure of a sentence, with its eye appeal, may seem to be merely an entertaining substitute for the "real" structure. But the visual structure is "real" also, as an alternative way of looking at the sentence. Moreover, it leads to a central issue about the sentence—its performance structure. Let me offer a few examples.

Here, to begin with, is the opening sentence of Boswell's *Life of Samuel Johnson* (1791), cast into a performance structure. It would work best if you read this sentence (and the other examples as well) aloud. I assume that you will make a pause (to taste) at the end of each line.

> To write the Life of him
>   who excelled all mankind
>   in writing the lives of others
>   and who
>   whether we consider his extraordinary endowments,
>   or his various works,
>   has been equalled by few in any age,
> is an arduous
>   and may be reckoned in me
>   a presumptuous task.

I believe that this kind of performance structure offers the several qualities that I mentioned in connection with visual structure—a stronger realization of organization, a greater sense of closure, deliberation in reading, and memorability. In addition to these qualities, the performance goes beyond eye appeal and brings in the appeal to the ear.

Here is another example to read aloud:

> It was that memorable day,
>   in the first summer of the late war,
>   when our navy engaged the Dutch;
> a day
>   wherein the two most mighty and best appointed fleets
>   which any age had ever seen
>   disputed
>   the command of the greater half of the globe,

the commerce of nations,
and the riches of the universe.

This performance structure focuses our attention on the narrative organization of the sentence: beginning with the *when* of it, moving on to the *wherein* of it, and concluding with the action, the *what* of it. We see and hear the elevated language in this burst of naval patriotism which anticipates the dramatic patriotism of the essay that follows. This is the first sentence of John Dryden's *An Essay of Dramatic Poesy* (1668).

In the afterglow of the passage that I quoted earlier from Donne's *Devotions,* please consider the following sentence. I quote it first in the form in which it was printed:

When we think how many millions of words have been written and printed in England in the past three hundred years, and how the vast majority have died out without leaving any trace, it is tempting to wonder what quality the words of Donne possess that we should still hear them distinctly today.

Here is the same sentence in a performance structure:

When we think
   how many millions of words
      have been written and printed in England
         in the past three hundred years,
      and how the vast majority
         have died out
            without leaving any trace,
   it is tempting to wonder
      what quality the words of Donne possess
         that we should still hear them
            distinctly
               today.

If this passage seriously tempts us to wonder about the quality of Donne's words, we have to notice that our wonder is that we still *hear* them distinctly today after the passage of three hundred years. Hearing them could be experienced only if we had met those words in some kind of performance, aloud. The structure in which I have cast his words—and those of the writer of this commentary—is at least a temptation to perform them, both now and later. The commentary we have been reading is the first sentence of the essay entitled "Donne After Three Centuries" in *The Second Common Reader* (1932), by Virginia Woolf. Here, from the same book, is the neat opening sentence of "The Niece of an Earl," cast into a performance structure and quoted here for the sheer pleasure of it:

> There is
> an aspect of fiction
> of so
> delicate
> a nature
> that less has been
> said about it
> than its importance
> deserves.

Doesn't the performance make you want to hear more about that particular aspect of fiction? It is, I think, the performance that creates the desire.

Here is one final example of performance structure. First, in the way in which it would normally appear in print:

> Besides these sovereign powers, divine and human, of which I have hitherto discoursed, there is mention in Scripture of another power, namely that of the rulers of the darkness of this world, the Kingdom of Satan and the Principality of Beelzebub over demons, that is to say, over phantasms that appear in the air: for which cause Satan is also called the Prince of the Power of the Air; and, because he ruleth in the darkness of this world, the Prince of this World: and in consequence hereunto, they who are under his dominion, in opposition to the faithful who are the Children of the Light are called the Children of Darkness.

It may seem odd to offer such a sentence as this one for performance. Its structure is rough and chopped up, and one thing in the sentence is made to lead to another only by the exertion of a little authorial pressure. But we cannot choose only well-wrought sentences for performance. We might prefer elegance, but other principles are important also in making the choice of what we will read and therefore perform. We will always be the losers, I think, if we try to cheat on an important text and get away with some form of familiarization other than a performance of it.

This is not part of a sermon, nor of a religious tract. Far from it. It is the opening sentence of Part IV, "Of the Kingdom of Darkness," of Thomas Hobbes's *Leviathan* (1651). Here is one way to put this sentence into a performance structure:

> Besides these sovereign powers, divine and human,
>> of which I have hitherto discoursed,
> there is mention in Scripture
>> of another power, namely
> that of the rulers of the darkness of this world,
>> the Kingdom of Satan and
>>> the Principality of Beelzebub
>>>> over demons, that is to say,
>>>> over phantasms that appear in the air:
>>>>> for which cause
> Satan is also called
>> the Prince of the Power of the Air; and
>>> because he ruleth in the darkness of this world,
>> the Prince of this World:
>>> and in consequence hereunto,
> they who are under his dominion,
>> in opposition to the faithful who are
>>> the Children of the Light
> are called
>> the Children of Darkness.

I do not mean to argue in favor of reprinting all our prose into performance structures, though it would doubtless help most of us to come to terms with some texts more easily if we had the convenience of a performing structure to guide us. I imagine that most really experienced readers do not have the need for such a convenience. At the best, they are like those expert musicians who can perform the most complex music at sight, even at first sight. The rest of us can at least try to move in that direction.

III

When English sentences are arranged in different ways, their impact generally varies also. Here is the opening sentence of Addison's *Spectator* No. 185 of October 2, 1711, with one alternate arrangement:

1. Men deceive themselves in nothing more than in what the World calls Zeal.

2. There is nothing in which Men more deceive themselves than in what the World calls Zeal.

The difference could doubtless be described in various ways. For one way: in the former, the first emphasis falls on "deceive themselves" while in the latter it falls on "nothing." The second emphasis within each sentence, which I think is less heavy in most performances, is the reverse: in the first it falls on "nothing" and in the second on "deceive themselves." The alternate structures thus yield a somewhat different impact because of what each emphasizes. Addison's own structure is the second of these two: "There is *NOTHING* in which Men more DECEIVE THEMSELVES than in what the WORLD calls ZEAL."

Here is the opening sentence of the "Conclusion" to Thoreau's *Walden*. Since the sentence has three main elements, six alternate versions are easily possible logically. If we put them all down, here is what they would look like:

1. The doctors wisely recommend a change of air and scenery to the sick.

2. The doctors wisely recommend to the sick a change of air and scenery.

3. A change of air and scenery the doctors wisely recommend to the sick.

4. A change of air and scenery to the sick the doctors wisely recommend.

5. To the sick the doctors wisely recommend a change of air and scenery.

6. To the sick a change of air and scenery the doctors wisely recommend.

Most readers would bridle at 4. and 6. on the grounds that they are not idiomatic. Many readers would probably feel uneasy about the idiomatic nature of 3. and 5. because that is probably not the way they speak. Which leaves 1. and 2. as comfortably straightforward statements composed of subject, verb, and objects.

What Thoreau wrote, however, was 5. This version of the sentence is a blunt beginning to a blunt conclusion. "The sick" are put up front to emphasize that it is they who need the change of air and scenery, just as it is we (according to Thoreau) who need new patterns of spirit and behavior.

Now for an example from Donne. This is the first sentence of the VIII Meditation. For a trial, I offer five versions of it and retain the spelling, capitalization, punctuation, and italicization of its appearance in the *Devotions upon Emergent Occasions* (1624).

1. We find new *discoveries* stil when we return to that *Meditation*, that *Man* is a *World*.

2. We find new *discoveries* in that *Meditation*, that *Man* is a *World*, stil when we return to it.

3. Stil when we return to that *Meditation*, that *Man* is a *World*, we find new *discoveries*.

4. In that *Meditation*, that *Man* is a *World*, we find new *discoveries* stil when we return to it.

5. In that *Meditation*, that *Man* is a *World*, stil when we return to it we find new *discoveries*.

There are, as you see, some five elements of prime importance in this sentence: the idea of finding, the idea of returning, the idea of meditation, the idea of man as a world, and the idea of new discoveries. Two of the versions begin by emphasizing the *finding* of new discoveries, one the *return* to a meditation, and two the *meditation* itself. That is only the beginning, of course. Each version goes ahead to put all five of the elements into a relationship with one another. The relationship of the elements is a little different in each version, and the relative importance of each element is accordingly a little different in each. There is perhaps more subtlety in the differences among these versions than in the earlier examples.

Donne's version was 3. We can readily see what thematic purpose that version serves—that even when we go back again and again to a fruitful idea, we can always make new discoveries.

Consider this final example of alternate versions. It is the opening sentence of Virginia Woolf's essay called "The 'Sentimental Journey'" in *The Second Common Reader* (1932). I offer eight alternate versions of the sentence:

1. Sterne wrote his first novel, *Tristram Shandy*, when he was forty-five years old, at a time when many have written their twentieth.

2. Sterne wrote his first novel, *Tristram Shandy*, at a time when many have written their twentieth, that is, when he was forty-five years old.

3. *Tristram Shandy*, though it is Sterne's first novel, was written when he was forty-five years old, at a time when many have written their twentieth.

4. *Tristram Shandy*, though it is Sterne's first novel, was written at a time when many have written their twentieth, that is, when he was forty-five years old.

5. When he was forty-five years old, when many have written their twentieth novel, Sterne wrote his first, *Tristram Shandy*.

6. When he was forty-five years old, Sterne wrote his first novel, *Tristram Shandy*, when many have written their twentieth.

7. At a time when many have written their twentieth novel, at the age of forty-five, Sterne wrote his first, *Tristram Shandy*.

8. At a time when many have written their twentieth novel, Sterne wrote his first, *Tristram Shandy*, at the age of forty-five.

Unlike the example from Thoreau, all eight of these versions seem to be entirely idiomatic. You could write or speak any one of them with comfort if the occasion were apt. For many purposes, one tells the story as well as another. Then why bother? No need to do so if any one of these texts will serve and satisfy.

Yet we can see, if we force ourselves to read and compare them with care, that each one creates a slightly different impression as to what is worth thinking about concerning Sterne's age when he wrote *Tristram Shandy*. Is it a matter of moment? It all depends. Perhaps yes, sometimes. Virginia Woolf's version was 4.

*   *   *   *

All kinds of thoughts may come into your head after looking at alternate structures of a sentence. Which is the "best" structure? Did I get it right in guessing which is the author's version? Is one of the alternate versions "better" than the one written by the author? This is the game-show way of looking at alternate structures, with prizes for all competitors. Fair enough.

Beyond that, the examples suggest the basic truth that a given sentence can generally take a number of structural forms, and the sentence as such can take a virtually unlimited number of structural forms. From each form, an effect that is different from that of each other one, different in greater or lesser degree. The effects of each of those forms can be defined and interpreted and explained. Since the process can be as elaborate as learning Zen through getting ready to shoot one arrow, I hope that each reader will kindly supply his or her own explanation.

IV

Sometimes the sentence has another kind of hidden structure. In this structure, the writer and the reader carry on a dialogue with one another. Since the interaction of this dialogue is like an exploratory searching for clarification, it seems convenient to call it the dialectic structure of the sentence.

This structure occurs, usually in relatively complicated sentences, when the reader is implicitly invited to become involved in the discussion. In his involvement, the reader begins to take part by asking questions or making comments, to which the writer responds. Or at least this is the effect that the structure creates, with a sense of dialectic and participation.

Here, for an example, is the first sentence of Sir Thomas Browne's *Religio Medici* (1643), cast into dialectic form, with the interior contribution of the reader—his or her thoughts or feelings—given a form of words:

The Writer	The Reader

The Writer

For my religion, though there be
several circumstances that might
persuade the world I have none
at all,

                The Reader

                What circumstances are
                those?

as the general scandal of my profession,
the natural course of my studies, the
indifferency of my behavior and discourse
in matters of religion,

                What do you mean by your
                "indifferency" in matters of
                religion?

neither violently defending one, nor
with that common ardor and contention
opposing another;

                Well, what claim do you
                make about your own
                religion?

yet, in despite hereof, I dare
without usurpation assume the
honorable style of a Christian.

Since what we as readers bring to the text is ourselves, many different kinds of participation are likely. I presented the reader of the Browne sentence in a noncommittal position as a seeker, and the sentence perhaps invites that position. But there are many other possibilities.

Here is the first sentence of Dryden's "Of Heroic Plays: An Essay" (1672), with a more contentious reader:

The Writer	The Reader

The Writer

Whether heroic verse ought to
be admitted into serious plays
is not now to be disputed:

                The Reader

                Why not? Why shouldn't we
                debate its admission?

'tis already in possession of
the stage,

> But is it there with the
> approval of the audience?

and I dare confidently affirm
that very few tragedies, in this
age, shall be received without
it.

The reader doesn't get very far debating with Dryden, at least in this sentence.

Here is the opening sentence of Part III ("Of a Christian Common-Wealth") of Hobbes's *Leviathan* (1651). This time I am supposing a polite reader:

The Writer	*The Reader*
I have derived the rights of sovereign power, and the duty of subjects hitherto, from the principles of nature only;	
	And what do you mean by "the principles of nature"?
such as experience has found true, or consent concerning words has made so;	
	I'm not sure what you mean. Would you say it again, please, in other words?
that is to say, from the nature of men, known to us by experience, and definitions (of such words as are essential to all political reasoning) universally agreed on.	
	Thank you. But I still don't understand.

For one more example, here are the first two sentences of Donne's VI Meditation from the *Devotions* (1624), putting the text into a performance structure, and supposing an inquisitive reader:

The Writer	*The Reader*
I observe the physician	
with the same diligence	
as he the disease;	

What do you see?

I see he fears,
  and I fear with him:

Do you fear much?

I overtake him,
  I overrun him in his fear and
I go the faster
  because he makes his pace slow;

Why do you fear so much?

I fear the more,
  because he disguises his fear and
I see it with the more sharpness
  because he would not have me see it.

Why does he hide his fear?
Will his fear harm his art?

He knows that his fear
  shall not disorder
    the practice and exercise
      of his art,

Then why does he hide his
fear?

but he knows that my fear
  may disorder
    the effect and working
      of his practice.

A good reason to hide his
fear.

These few examples of dialectic structure can be multiplied almost indefinitely, and from all centuries. It occurs most often whenever the structure of the sentence invites (or simply permits) the reader to become involved in the argument that is being put forth. This involvement leads then to the structure of a hidden dialogue between the writer and the reader, and that structure greatly influences the way the reader understands the text.

You may not be the noncommittal reader I have supposed for Browne, or the contentious reader of Dryden, or the polite reader of Hobbes, or the inquisitive reader of Donne. But each one of us is some kind of reader. And when the structure leads us to perform a text with our own special understanding, we bring our own dialectic to the text.

V

Mr. Shandy was right. No brain is so barren but an unlimited number of sentences can issue forth from it. And those sentences can be of an infinite variety.

Seeing sentences in performance structure can remind us, visually, what a wide range of patterns the English language offers us, and what complexity. Seeing alternative arrangements of a few sentences can remind us of the rich subtlety of the different patterns in their effect on us. Seeing a few sentences in dialectic structure can remind us how much we can be drawn into the web of the discourse in the pattern of the sentence.

Most of all, the variety and the richness.

And how our understanding is different as we respond to each one of them.

4.

THE MUSIC OF THE WORD
The Sound of the Sentence

In earlier centuries, when reading was more likely to be aloud, the sound of the sentence was a natural part of its total effect. Those of us who try to achieve a full understanding of texts will profit by listening to the sound of the sentence in our performance of most prose before this century, and of much prose in our own times as well. Even when the reading is silent, as it generally is now, and as it has been increasingly so for some centuries, the music of the word still makes some kind of contribution to our understanding of the text.

In the last chapter, I suggested several different ways of thinking about the structure of the sentence. One of them grew out of putting a sentence into a performance structure and reading it aloud. The appeal was then to the ear as well as to the eye.

In this chapter, I would like to offer some further examples of prose in performance structure in order to open up some additional ways of thinking about the appeal that prose makes to our understanding, this time through its music. First, a few examples to suggest the basic elements of the rhythm of English prose, and a quick review of the chief methods that have been used in the past to try to deal with or appreciate the rhythm of prose. Next, I will review a few short passages, from the 17th century to our own time: by reading them, I hope that we can get some further hints about the range of ways in which the sound of the sentence creates its effect on us. Finally, I would like to offer several sentences, from the 16th century to the present time, in which the rhythm may seem less familiar: these, too, may offer insights about the music of English prose, or about the ways that we read it.

I

I begin with two sentences from a single book. One is the opening of the first chapter, and the other is the next to the last paragraph of the whole book. Here they are in the way they normally look:

1. God, whome the wisest men acknowledge to be a power uneffable, and vertue infinite, a light by abundant claritie invisible, an understanding which it selfe can onely comprehend, an essence eternall and spirituall, of absolute purenesse and simplicitie, was and is pleased to make himselfe knowne by the worke of the World: in the wonderfull magnitude whereof, (all which he imbraceth, filleth, and sustaineth) we behold the image of that glorie, which cannot bee measured, and withall that one, and yet universall nature, which cannot be defined.

2. O eloquent, just and mightie Death! whom none could advise, thou hast perswaded; what none hath dared, thou hast done; and whom all the world hath flattered, thou only has cast out of the world and despised: thou hast drawne together all the pride, crueltie, and ambition of man, and covered it over with these two narrow words, *Hic jacet.*

And here they are in a performance structure, as I read them. The acute accents show where I put primary emphasis, and the (infrequent) grave accents show my secondary emphasis. Occasionally, in my reading, the emphasis may fall on two words jointly, or on a short phrase; I indicate this by a line above the words. Let me say again that this is my own performance, and other readers may perform these passages in a somewhat different way. No matter. The principles that we explore will, I believe, be the same.

1. Gód, whome the wísest mén acknówledge to bé
    a pówer unéffable, and vértue ínfinite,
    a líght by abúndant cláritie invísible,
    an understánding which it sélfe can ónely comprehénd,
    an éssence etérnall and spírituall,
    of ábsolute púrenesse and simplícitie,
  wás and ís plèased to make himselfe knowne
    by the wórke of the Wórld:
        in the wónderfull mágnitude whereóf,

(áll which he imbráceth, fílleth, and sustáineth)
we behóld
the ímage of that glórie,
which cánnot bee méasured,
and witháll that óne, and yet univérsall náture,
which cánnot be defíned.

2. O éloquent, júst and míghtie Déath!
whom nóne could advíse,
thóu hast perswáded;
what nóne hath dáred,
thóu hast dóne;
and whom all the world hath fláttered,
thóu ònly has cást out of the wórld and despísed:
thóu hast dráwne togèther
áll the farre stretched gréatnesse,
áll the príde, cruéltie, and ambítion of mán,
and cóvered it óver with thése twò nárrow wórds,
Híc jácet.

The accent marks visualize (at least in a crude way) what is emphasized and what is not, and thereby suggest the rhythm of the passages. Or rather the rhythms, as the rhythm of almost every line is a little different from that of each of the others— which is generally true of English prose. The more lapse of time there is between emphases, the lighter the rhythmic effect tends to be. Consider the first line: "Gód, whŏme tĥe wísĕst mén ăcknówlĕdge tŏ ƀe." Its moderately heavy rhythm includes two time-lapses with two unaccented syllables, and two with one. None of the lines in these passages are notably light, but consider the effect of the fourth line of the first passage—"ăn ŭndĕrstándiñg whĭch ĭt sélfe căn ónely cŏmprĕhénd": three unaccented syllables in three cases, and one in the fourth. The result is a light rhythm that ripples along. Compare that with the end of the second passage, "thése twò nárrŏw wórds, / *Híc jácĕt*": six heavy emphases, with only two unaccented syllables to lighten the effect. The virtual absence of time-lapses between the naturally heavy emphases creates a staccato rhythm and a massive, overwhelming effect.

The book from which these passages are taken is *The History of the World* (1614), by Sir Walter Raleigh. These are grave, serious matters that Raleigh is treating with such solemnity.

For a less weighty matter in a lighter manner, consider this sentence:

> Gentle reader, I presume thou wilt be very inquisitive to know what antic or personate actor this is that so insolently intrudes upon this common theatre to the world's view, arrogating another man's name, whence he is, why he doth it, and what he hath to say.

And here is the sentence in a performance structure:

> Géntle réader,
> I presúme thou wilt be véry inquísitive to knów
>   what ántic or pérsonate áctor thìs ís
>   that so ínsolently intrúdes
>   upon this cómmon théatre to the wórld's víew,
>   árrogating anóther man's náme,
>   whénce he ís,
>   whý he dóth it,
>   and whát he háth to sáy.

The rhythm is consistently lighter than it was in Raleigh. The pattern of the rhythm in this sentence has a modest range of time lapses between the emphases, but preponderantly of one or two syllables. Of course it is not just the number of syllables that matters, but the length of the syllables and also the time that we choose to take to speak them, or the time-lapse between the emphases.

This passage is the opening sentence of "Democritus Junior to the Reader," with which Robert Burton begins his *Anatomy of Melancholy* (1621). It shares with the passages from Raleigh a great deal of parallelism of structure, which is made more evident by arranging the passages into a performance structure. Raleigh develops the subject of his first sentence, for example, by putting five attributes of God into parallel structure, and Burton concludes his opening sentence with three parallel questions about the speaker.

It is obvious that different readers will perform these passages in different ways, depending on their understanding of the passages and on their experience and skill. In the past, our community of literary scholars has often considered performance as the unliterary purview of public speaking teachers or (in an earlier age) elocutionists. We have not always recognized that performance and reading both depend on and reveal our understanding of the text, and (reciprocally) that we come to understand the text by learning to perform it.

Before trying to develop ideas about the sound of the sentence through a discussion of a variety of kinds of examples, I would like to offer a short digression on the two most usual methods of dealing with the rhythm of prose and to explain why I believe they would not be fruitful for me to use in carrying on the discussion that makes up this chapter.

One way is to treat the rhythm of prose in the manner in which we have learned, from the classical tradition, to treat the rhythm of verse. That is, divide a passage into feet, scan it by marking the accented and unaccented syllables, and name the metres that result—iambic, trochaic, and all the rest. Essentially, prose is thus treated like verse on the grounds that it is thought to have regular recurrence of accented syllables. The most notable practitioner of this method was George Saintsbury (*History of English Prose Rhythm*, 1912), who resurrected many out-of-the-way metres (amphibrach, molossus, epitrites, paeons, proceleusmatic, and the rest) to give some kind of order to what would otherwise be relative chaos. Saintsbury had several important predecessors, including Aristotle: although Aristotle asserted (*The Art of Rhetoric*, III.viii) that prose should *not* be metrical, he went on to say that it should have rhythm; and he then gave metrical names used for verse to the different kind of rhythm (heroic, iambic, trochaic, and paeons). The mere mention of these terms by Aristotle gave later writers the encouragement they wanted to do a metrical analysis of prose. The metrical method is still sometimes used by writers on prose: it offers a vocabulary and a way to satisfy our desire for order. In my opinion, it works only on rigorously selected passages, and it is not of general value in helping us to understand the whole range of the rhythms of prose.

A variation of this method is the *cursus*, the system of rhythmical clause endings used in medieval Latin and brought up to date by several writers of this century, notably by Morris W. Croll in "The Cadence of English Oratorical Prose" (1919, and included in his *Style, Rhetoric, and Rhythm,* Princeton, 1966, with very useful references to the earlier scholarship). The cadenced endings fall into four Latin metres (*planus, tardus, velox, trispon-daic*), all counted backwards from the conclusion. Croll added English variations to these metres, and discovered examples of the *cursus* not only in the Authorized Version of the Bible and in Collects but also at the ends of clauses in oratorical prose. While this variation is an interesting adaptation of metrical scanning, I believe that its value is actually very limited and that even then the results depend on the ingenuity of the analyst in creating metres to fit our natural prose rhythms.

The other way is to treat prose as if it were song and to create a time notation for it as in a musical score. This method also derives from a way of treating verse, under a theory of prosody based on musical notation. Some of the modern practitioners of that theory are Joshua Steele (1775), Edwin Guest (1838), Sidney Lanier (1880), William Thomson (1923), and Morris W. Croll (1929/1966), all of whose works are discussed in the Croll book mentioned above. Those who treat prose under this theory tend to consider it as an accessory or adjunct form of the language of poetry, but with pleasure that it seems to share this feature with verse. In my opinion, the advantages of attempting to apply time notations to prose are more satisfying in theory than in practice: as with the metrical method, it works only for rigorously selected passages, and I do not learn much from it. The very interesting work of phoneticians and psychologists on the speaking of language has a bearing on the time notation theory of prosody. Many studies have revealed details about how we read, how our actual practice differs from what we think we do, how we differ from one another in all the details that go to make up speech rhythm. References to significant studies along these lines are included in D. W. Harding's *Words into Rhythm: English Speech Rhythm in Verse and Prose* (Cambridge, 1976). Finally, many thoughtful comments on the metrical and musical and speech methods of dealing with prose (and references to earlier scholarship) are contained in *The Other Harmony of Prose,* by Paull Franklin Baum (Duke, 1952). Those who want to read a long, discursive, speculative account of the theory of rhythm may find Henri Meschonnic's *Critique du Rythme* (Paris, Verdier, 1982) just to their taste. Thus endeth the Digression.

II

The rhythm of English prose depends on how the text is read. I have been suggesting, to begin with, that rhythm (which is established by the time-lapses between emphases) can be simply identified by marking emphases as for reading. Then one can notice whether the emphases are heavy or light, what kind of time-lapses separate them, and what other effects are created. It is, I think, pointless to divide passages into feet and scan them, and misleading to set them to music. But there are other features to be observed within the pattern of rhythm.

Let us go back to looking at a few familiar passages, and then reading them in a performance structure with emphasis marked. This is neither a metrical nor a musical reading. We are not limited to a set pattern of metre nor to a set pattern of time notation, both of which encourage the search for recurrence even at the risk of distorting our natural way of reading a text. Let me say again that the accents mark only my sense of where the emphases fall. Here is one passage, in its usual form:

> What Song the *Syrens* sang, or what name *Achilles* assumed
> when he hid himself among women, though puzling
> Questions, are not beyond all conjecture. What time the
> persons of these Ossuaries entred the famous Nations of
> the dead, and slept with Princes and Counsellours, might
> admit a wide solution. But who were the proprietaries of
> these bones, or what bodies these ashes made up, were a
> question above Antiquarism. Not to be resolved by man,
> nor easily perhaps by spirits, except we consult the Pro-
> vinciall Guardians, or tutellary Observators.

And here it is in a performance structure:

> What Sóng the *Sýrens* sáng,
> or what náme *Achílles* assúmed
> when he híd himsèlf among wómen,
> though púzling Quéstions,
> are nót beyònd áll conjécture.
> What tíme the pérsons of thèse Ossúaries
> éntred the fámous Nátions of the déad,
> and slépt with Prínces and Cóunsellours,
> might admít a wíde solútion.

But whó were the propríetaries of thèse bónes,
or whát bódies thèse áshes made up,
were a qúestion abóve Antiqúarism.
Nót to be resólved by mán,
nor eásily perháps by spírits,
excépt we consúlt the Provínciall Guárdians,
or tútellary Obsérvators.

We are talking about rhythm. It is evident that this passage—
from Sir Thomas Browne's *Hydriotaphia, Urn Burial* (1658), the
fourth paragraph of the last chapter—sounds rhythmical when
you read it aloud. It even begins with a regular iambic line, which
is an auspicious opening for the confirmed metrist. But thereafter all is metrical chaos. Although the passage could be divided
into feet and names assigned to each, the result would be a
hodgepodge of names; and it would be equally idle to divide it
into measures and assign time values to each syllable, a quarter
note here, a dotted eighth note there. Still, the flow of the passage
sounds rhythmical, despite the fact that it does not submit quietly
to the usual analyses.

If we look at its patterns of accents, we see that in almost
three-quarters of the cases the time-lapse between accents is represented by one or two syllables. The time-lapse for a few is three
or four syllables, and a few have none at all. If we trust our ears,
we will accept this kind of pattern as one that contributes to a
feeling of rhythm for this particular passage. We hear the recurrence of emphasis within a pattern of sound, and within the
recurrences we perceive a pattern of rhythm.

There are, of course, other features that contribute to the
music. One is the close recurrence of sounds in the passage.
Consider the first three lines:

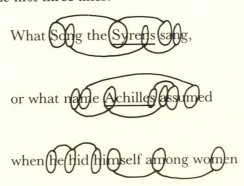

In the first line, there is alliteration on the *n* sound, and consonance in the pattern of the repetition of the *s* sound with the shifts in the following vowels; in the second line, alliteration on the *m* and *s*, and assonance on the *a* sound; and in the third, alliteration on the *h* and *m* sounds. Since the reader hears these recurrences without being poked in the ribs by the analyst, I will not continue to call special attention to the details of the internal sound patterns.

One other feature that always contributes to the music of prose is the inflection that we use in our reading—the rise and fall in the pitch of our voices, the subtle intonation that we give as we move from one word to the next in our reading. It would not do, however, to indicate the music of our reading of prose by real musical notation, with an absolute pitch given each word or syllable: in reading, we do not jump from one pitch to another by intervals and create a melody, but rather slide from one tone to another through any intervening tones. Moreover, the natural pitches of our voices may differ a lot, as may the amount that our voices rise and fall in reading, our tempi and pauses, and the amount of our emphases and holding words in our reading.

Let me put these same three lines from *Hydriotaphia* into a form—or the mere suggestion of a form—to convey an outline of the inflection that I give in reading the passage:

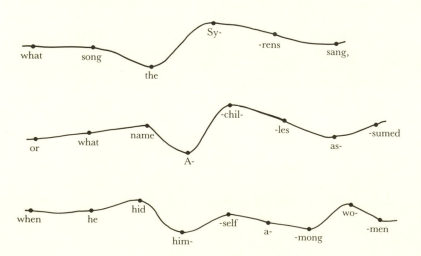

Other people will doubtless use a different inflection in reading the same passage. The only reason for giving this example is to emphasize the fact that our reading—our inflection—is always a part of the music of the word.

You may feel that I have been singling out "poetic" prose in the examples I have so far offered, all from the musical 17th century. Let me offer a couple of examples that are not normally considered "poetic," from the following hundred years or so. Here they are in their usual form:

1. These are the times that try men's souls. The summer soldier and the sunshine patriot will in this crisis, shrink from the service of his country; but he that stands it *now,* deserves the love and thanks of man and woman. Tyranny, like hell, is not easily conquered; yet we have this consolation with us, that the harder the conflict, the more glorious the triumph. What we obtain too cheap, we esteem too lightly; it is dearness only that gives everything its value.

2. The eye that can prefer the Colouring of Titian and Rubens to that of Michael Angelo and Rafael, ought to be modest and to doubt its own powers.

And here they are in a performance structure, with my emphases indicated:

1. Thése are the tímes that trý men's sóuls.
   The súmmer sóldier and the súnshine pátriot wíll
       in thís crísis,
     shrínk from the sérvice of his cóuntry;
   but he that stands it *nów,*
       desérves the lóve and thánks of mán and wóman.
   Týranny, like héll, is not éasily cónquered;
     yet we have thís consolátion wíth ùs,
       that the hárder the cónflict,
       the more glórious the tríumph.
   What we obtáin too chéap,
   we estéem too líghtly;
       it is déarness ónly
       that gives éverything its válue.

2. The éye that can prefér the Cólouring
      of Títian and Rúbens
      to thát of Míchael Àngelo and Ráfael,
    óught to be módest
    and to dóubt its ówn pówers.

The first passage is highly rhythmical. There is a great deal of regularity in the recurrence of the rhythms, and heavy emphases on the key words and phrases. And it uses the reinforcement of alliteration, with a vengeance: it is the *t* sound of the first line and the *s* sound of the next three that make it grab the reader with such ferocity. Through the remainder of the passage, antithesis governs all and makes a melodramatic appeal. This is the beginning of Thomas Paine's *The Crisis*, No. I (1776). To most ears, it now sounds mannered and artificial. Such is the fate of prose in which the intrinsic qualities (whether of sound or structure or whatever) are pushed to their limits in order to create an especially strong effect. The final rhetorical risk is the risk of unintended laughter.

The second little passage is also notably rhythmical, with a pattern of agreeable time-lapses between the accents. The light running rhythm carries you along up to the last few words, when the climax of the passage is reached. The climax is a series of heavy emphases, with very brief time-lapses. The rhythm of the passage ends by creating a kind of attack on that foolish eye with which it opens. This is the first sentence of the Preface to William Blake's *Descriptive Catalogue of Pictures* (1809).

The following two passages, written in the 19th century, may tell us something (especially when put into performance structure) about the way that rhythm is affected by the pauses and the emphases that we make in our reading, and our consequent reactions:

1. It is nòt éasy
      to wríte a famíliar stýle.
      <u>Many people</u> mistáke a famíliar
        for a vúlgar stýle,
        and suppóse that to wríte without áffectátion
          is to wríte at rándom.
      On the cóntrary,
        there is nóthing that requíres more

precísion,
aǹd, if I may só sáy,
púrity of expréssion,
than the stýle I am spéaking òf.

2. Áll wórk, even cótton-spínning,
    is nóble;
wórk is alóne nóble: be thát hère sáid
    and assérted once móre.
And in líke mánner, toò, all dígnity
    is páinful;
a lífe of éase is nót for ány màn,
    nor for ány gód.
The lífe of áll góds fígures itsélf to ús as
    a Sublíme Sádness,—
éarnestness of Ínfinite Báttle against
    Ínfinite Lábour.
Our híghest relígion is námed
    the 'Wórship of Sórrow.'

The internal structure of the first passage leads us to pause after a relatively few words, read on and pause, sometimes breathe, move on deliberately, pause again, think about what is being said, and turn it over quietly in our minds. The language is strongly assertive and self-confident, but the structural rhythm gives the passage a cast of meditation. It is the beginning of William Hazlitt's essay "On Familiar Style" (1821).

The rhythm of the second passage is dominated by a frequent, heavy beat with relatively few time-lapses between the emphases. The effect of the rhythm is grave and ponderous. The obvious impression that comes from reading this passage is that the emphases are falling close together. This is an impression that can be quickly validated by noting the ratio of accented to unaccented syllables. The ratio in this passage is about a quarter higher than in the first passage, and higher than in any of the passages I have quoted except the Raleigh passage on death. This passage is the beginning of Book III, chapter IV of Thomas Carlyle's *Past and Present* (1843).

I am sure that some readers would have been glad to see a set of tables with detailed quantification of the units that establish the rhythms within a given passage, as Josephine Miles did for the parts of speech—the percentages of adjectives, nouns, verbs, and connectives in representative passages from several hundred writers—in her *Eras & Modes in English Poetry* (1957) and *Style and Proportion* (1967). I am sorry that I cannot oblige. I have tried to reduce some of the features of all the passages I quote (and many others as well) to some meaningful numerical order: such as the ratio of emphases to unaccented syllables in each passage, and the percentage of each kind of unit rhythm in each passage. The results were, in my opinion, meaningless, and I have spared the reader having to look at them. I have contented myself with offering a few words about whatever features of each passage seemed to me significant.

I would like to conclude this section with two short 20th century passages, put into performance structure:

1. The évil done by Ste Béuve
   is consíderable and incálculable.
   It has allówed évery párasite and nítwìt
      to presént himsélf as a crític,
   and thóusands of éssayists
      incápable of understánding a mán's wórk or his génius
         have found opportúnity in a discússion of wásh lísts.

2. Críticism,
      I táke it,   ̗
   is the fórmal díscourse of an amateur.
   When there is enóugh lóve and enóugh knówledge
         represénted in the díscourse
      it is a sélf-suffícient but by no means an ísolated árt.
   It wítnesses cónstantly in its ówn life
         its ínterdepéndence with the óther árts.
   It lays out the térms and párallels of appreciátion
         from the óutside ín
      in órder to convíct itself of intérnal íntimacy;
   it námes and arránges what it knóws and lóves,
      and séarches éndlessly with évery frésh ímpulse or
      impréssion   ̗
         for bétter námes and more orderly arrángements.

The dominant rhythm of the first passage is that of a two-syllable time-lapse between emphases. The beat is light—in fact, lighter than any of the passages I have quoted. The smooth rhythm throws the emphasis on those accents without time-lapses between them. Thus those words call attention to themselves and serve as internal climaxes—nítwìt, / mán's wórk, / wásh lísts. The rhythmic effect is that of attack, like the Blake passage. This is the beginning of the essay "Harold Monro," reprinted as the first essay in Ezra Pound's *Polite Essays* (1937).

The dominant rhythm of the second passage is that of a one-syllable time-lapse—tȟe fórmăl díscŏurse, / tȟe óthĕr árts, / cŏnvíct ĭtsélf. But the rhythm is greatly varied. The ear is offended by too much regularity of rhythm in prose. As Aristotle said, prose should not be metrical. When prose falls into a more or less regular metre, we are usually puzzled if we notice it. For example, T. H. Huxley's "On a Piece of Chalk" (1868 as a lecture, 1880 as an essay) begins as follows:

Ĭf ă wéll wĕre súnk ăt oŭr féet
ĭn tȟe mídst ŏf tȟe cítў ŏf Nórwĭch. . . .

This anapestic trimeter is entirely regular except for a substitution of an iamb in the second foot and a feminine ending for the second line. If you stopped right there in your reading, what would the rhythm have led you to expect? Something comic, surely—and certainly not a serious discourse on geology.

Back to the passage on criticism, with the variety around its dominating rhythm, such as: aňd séarchĕs éndlĕsslў wíth évеrў frésh ímpŭlse ŏr ĭmpréssĭon—where the time-lapses are 1, 1, 3, 1, 0, 3, 1—and they are all blended together. The passage as a whole gives the sense of variety with an underlying regularity. What counts for more is the variety within the breathing unit. And what counts for most is the effectiveness to the ear of the euphonious variety that makes up the rhythm. This passage is the beginning of "A Critic's Job of Work," the last essay in R. P. Blackmur's *The Double Agent* (1935).

III

The music of much of our prose strikes the ear with less of the sense of rhythmic regularity than that created by the quotations in the preceding section. Sometimes the writer may be less competent than this group of stars from which I quoted, ranging in time from Sir Thomas Browne to R. P. Blackmur. Sometimes, however, the different kind of music may have a different cause and a different effect.

I would like to offer a few examples of good English prose that presents some other varieties of music. To begin with, here is an example from Edmund Spenser. It is his explanatory preface to *The Faerie Queene* (1590); he cast this explanation—in which beginning students of Spenser find much comfort—in the form of a letter to Sir Walter Raleigh. This is its opening sentence:

> Sir knowing how doubtfully all Allegories may be construed, and this booke of mine, which I have entituled the Faery Queene, being a continued Allegory, or darke conceit, I have thought good as well for avoyding of gealous opinions and misconstructions, as also for your better light in reading thereof, (being so by you commanded,) to discover unto you the general intention and meaning, which in the whole course thereof I have fashioned, without expressing of any particular purposes or by-accidents therein occasioned.

And here it is in a performance structure, to be read aloud:

Sír knówing how dóubtfully
   àll Állegories may be constrúed,
     and thìs boòke of mìne,
        which I have entítuled thè Fáery Quéene,
           béing a contínued Állegory, or dárke concéit,
   I have thoùght goòd as wéll for avóyding
     géalous opínions and mísconstrúctions,
   as álso for your bétter líght in réading theréof,
   (bèing só by yóu commánded,)
        to discóver únto yòu the géneral inténtion and méaning,
          whìch in the whóle cóurse theréof I have fáshioned,
     withoùt expréssing of ány partícular púrposes
        or bý-áccidents therein occásioned.

The rhythm is noticeably different from that of the earlier passages. One key to the difference is the large number of emphases that come together, without any intervening time-lapse, like: àll Állegories, thìs boòke, thóught góod, beìng só, whóle cóurse. These emphases are not, for the most part, on key words, and they do not create a strong effect as they do at the end of the passage about death that I quoted from Raleigh, or even the last words of the one from Blake. Another difference is the varied time-lapses between emphases, without much audible recurrence, in many parts of the passage, as: béiňg ă cŏntínuĕd Állĕgŏrÿ, ŏr dárke cŏncéit—where the time-lapses between emphases are three syllables, one, four, and one. On the other hand, the recurrences create a strong rhythm in some parts, as in: géalŏus ŏpíniŏns ănd míscŏnstrúctiŏns, with the repeated two-syllable and then the repeated one-syllable time-lapses. But the total effect is a mixed music.

Here is another passage to practise on. For the fun of it, I won't identify the writer at the outset.

> Had those, who would perswade us, that there are innate Principles, not taken them together in gross; but considered, separately, the parts, out of which those Propositions are made, they would not, perhaps, have been so forward to believe they were innate. Since, if the *Ideas*, which made up those Truths, were not, it was impossible, that the Propositions, made up of them, should be innate, or our Knowledge of them be born with us.

And here is the passage in a performance structure for reading aloud:

Had thóse, who would perswáde ùs,
    that there áre innáte Prínciples,
        nót taken them together in gross;
    but consídered, séparately, the párts,
        out of which thóse Propositions are máde,
    they would nót, perhàps, have been só fórward
    to belíeve they wère innáte.
Sìnce, if the *Idéas*, which made up those Trúths, were nót,
    it was impóssible, that the Propositions, made up of them,
    shóuld bè innáte,
    or our Knówledge of them be bórn with us.

Several rhythmic features stand out in this passage. That a lot of heavy accents herd together with relatively little rest between them, like: nót taken them together in gross *or* Prŏpŏsítiŏns, made up of them, shóuld bè ĭnnáte. A Renaissance rhetorician might have said that this is the clenched fist of logic rather than the open hand of persuasion. Also, the recurrence of rhythmic units is so limited that no pattern emerges, or even much sense of rhythm. For another feature, that the parts of the passage between natural pauses for breathing are rather long. Indeed, I confess that I find it very difficult to decide where those pauses should fall. You may respond by saying that the author didn't write his book to be read aloud. No matter. Where to pause is an issue whether the reading is silent or aloud. Reading the passage aloud can reveal more clearly the internal structure and organization. Reading it aloud also makes manifest the music of the prose, which is there anyway and runs in our understanding if not in our ears. The passage is (if you don't already know) the beginning of Book I, chapter IV of John Locke's *An Essay Concerning Human Understanding* (1690).

Here is a passage which raises another kind of question about the music of prose. Please read the following sentence in any way that satisfies you:

> It must not be supposed, that, in the remarks I have made in the foregoing Discourse on the organic character (if I may use so strong a word in want of a better) of the various branches of Knowledge, viewed together, that I have been merely pointing out a peculiarity, which we may recognize or not at our pleasure; and that, on the ground, for instance, that a System of knowledge is more beautiful intellectually, or more serviceable in practice, true though this may be, than a confused litter of facts, or a heap of observations or rules.

For most readers, the music of this passage will seem quiet and far-off, in a way that is not true for most readings of the passages I quoted in the earlier sections. To some, it will perhaps sound choppy or confused. If you were able to read the sentence to your satisfaction, please say how the music sounded to you.

It is difficult for me to put this passage into a satisfactory performance structure because of the many alternate places where a reader may or may not choose to pause. Here is an effort at doing so:

It must nót be suppósed,
  thàt, in the remárks I have máde in my foregóing Díscourse
  on the orgánic cháracter
    (if I may úse so stróng a wórd in wánt of a bétter)
  of the várious bránches of Knówledge, víewed togéther,
  that I have been mérely pointing out a peculiárity,
  which we may récognize or nót at our pléasure;
  and thát, on the gróund, for ínstance,
  that a Sýstem of knówledge is more béautiful intelléctually
  or more sérviceable in práctice,
    trúe though thís may bé,
  than a confúsed lítter of fácts,
  or a héap of observátions or rúles.

When I read the passage again in this form, the music becomes
clearer for me. I hear the rising rhythm (one or two syllables
before an emphasis) that dominates the beginning and the middle of the lines, like: Ĭt mŭst nót bĕ sŭppósed *or* ŏf tñe várĭoŭs
bránchĕs ŏf Knówlĕdge. I also hear the falling rhythm (one, two,
or three syllables after an emphasis) that dominates the end of
the lines, like: víewed tŏgéthĕr, *or* ăt ŏur pléasŭre. Each of the
last three lines, however, ends firmly with an emphasis. A clear
pattern of rhythm emerges in the sentence if we pay attention to
performing it sympathetically.

I think that this passage is an interesting example of the fact
that performance helps to realize the structure and gives life to
the implicit music of the text. The passage is the opening sentence of Discourse VI of Newman's *Discourses on the Scope and
Nature of University Education* (1852).

I would like to offer the following passage as one last example
of a further variety of the music of prose:

> So we think of Marilyn who was every man's love affair
> with America, Marilyn Monroe who was blonde and beau-
> tiful and had a sweet little rinky-dink of a voice and all
> the cleanliness of all the clean American backyards. She
> was our angel, the sweet angel of sex, and the sugar of
> sex came up from her like a resonance of sound in the
> clearest grain of a violin. Across five continents the men
> who knew the most about love would covet her, and the
> classical pimples of the adolescent working his first gas

pump would also pump for her, since Marilyn was deliverance, a very Stradivarius of sex, so gorgeous, forgiving,
humorous compliant and tender that even the most me-
diocre musician would relax his lack of art in the dissolv-
ing magic of her violin.

This passage, unlike the last two examples, almost begs to be put
into a performance structure. Here is a suggestion of the way
that I read it aloud:

So we thìnk of Márilyn
   who was évery mán's lóve affaìr with América,
Márilyn Monróe
   who was blónde and beáutiful
      and had a swéet lìttle rínky-dìnk of a vóice
      and áll the cléanliness of áll the cléan Américan
         báckyàrds.
Shé was oùr ángel,
   the swéet ángel of séx,
      and the súgar of séx came úp from hèr
      like a résonance of sóund
         in the cléarest gráin of a violín.
Across fíve cóntinents
   the mén who knéw the móst about lóve
      would cóvet hér,
   and the clássical pímples of the adoléscent wórking his
      fírst gás pùmp
      would álso púmp for hèr,
         since Márilyn wás delíverance,
   a véry Stradivárius of séx,
      so górgeous, forgíving, húmorous
      complíant and ténder
         that éven the mòst mediócre musícian
            would reláx his láck of árt
               in the dissólving mágic of her violín.

What to say first? That the music of this passage has a very
heavy beat. It is loaded with emphasis. The only other passages
that I have quoted in this chapter with such a large ratio of
emphases to syllables are Raleigh's passage on death, and Car-

lyle's on the nobility of work. The present passage joins those two in trying to make a strong, forceful presentation.

The passage on Marilyn Monroe is so emphatic that it does not create the effect of having a recurrent rhythm that the ear can hear, though of course it has lots of graceful little rhythms with one or two time-lapses separating the emphases, as in the first two lines: Sŏ wĕ thĭnk ŏf Márĭlȳn / wĥo wăs évĕry mán's lóve ăffáir wĭth Ămérĭcă.

But it is the heavy beat that dominates the entire passage. There are a good many examples of emphases without separation, like: báckyàrds, oùr ángĕl, swéet ángĕl, fírst gás pùmp. But the device that gives even greater strength to the beat is alliteration, as in such phrases as: *b*londe and *b*eautiful, *r*inky-dink,*s*ugar of *s*ex, *S*tradivarius of *s*ex, *m*ost *m*ediocre *m*usician, re*lax* his *lac*k, and *M*arilyn *M*onroe itself. ("Sugar of sex" can be noted as a wonderfully meaningless phrase that is, to adopt its own tactic, shoved into seeming sense by its sound.)

In short, this is strong writing, though essentially trashy. It is the music of the words that contributes most of all to its effect, and that music bears a resemblance to its contemporaneous music of the Rolling Stones. The passage is (though you may have known it all along) the first sentence of Norman Mailer's *Marilyn a biography* (1973).

IV

The various passages that I have quoted in this chapter give only a bare suggestion of the range of the music of English prose. The fact is that every piece of prose has its own music, its own private, individual fingerprint of sound. So far as the music goes, prose resists our love of categorizing, of naming the parts, of preparing a manual on disassembly and assembly. We need to think about each one in its own terms.

The features that we can look for are relatively simple and straightforward. Most of all, we have to tune our ears to the music of prose and to trust our ears. Every piece turns out to be a new experience and a new adventure in reading and performance. The rhythm and the sound become part of the way we understand the piece.

Most of us have a predisposition in favor of a rhythm that combines regularity and variety. The passages from Raleigh and

Burton, quoted in the first section of this chapter, are examples that are rhythmically pleasing to the ears of most of us, even though the rhetoric seems old-fashioned. The examples in the second section, beginning with Sir Thomas Browne and concluding with Blackmur, illustrate something of the range of rhythm that seems naturally pleasing to most readers of our time. That range of pleasing probably includes the music that moves to melodiousness in Browne, to melodrama in Paine, to snappishness in Blake, to meditativeness in Hazlitt, to ponderousness in Carlyle, to attack in Pound, to openness in Blackmur.

But what about other writings that do not seem to fit so comfortably into that kind of pattern of regular rhythm? The passage from Spenser, with its mixture of close emphases and strong rhythms. Or the passage from Locke, with its long breathings, heavy accents, and lack of grace. Or the passage from Newman, with the deep uncertainty about how to perform it. These have their music too, though it may not be like the songs of spring. Different ears with different cultures hear and create different sounds that they respond to as music.

The more we are removed in our culture from the natural habit of reading prose aloud to one another, the more likely it becomes that the music of prose will fall into a greater variety of patterns. And some of those patterns will seem strange to our unaccustomed ears. Some writers, like Locke, tend naturally to direct their appeals to the eye and to the mind. But the ear is always involved, so long as the medium is language. And the music may become increasingly complex as we listen to it.

The music of the word is, first of all and last of all, an appeal to our sense of hearing: the more we hear, the richer the music. We must trust our ears to hear the sound of the sentence.

Echo:

> Wĕ mŭst trŭst oŭr eárs tŏ héar
> the sóund ŏf thĕ séntĕnce.

5.

THE POWER OF THE WORD
Choice and Context

In the use of language, the first choice we have to make is words. All else comes later. The native speaker gets many clues from noticing the words that are chosen. If we hear *purchase* when the normal word to use is *buy*, we know something unusual is going on. In due course, we may know what it is. The speaker may be trying to impress us, or may be making a little joke, or may be disposed (for some reason or other) to the use of inflated language, or something else. We may find out.

In reading, similar problems arise, though they are usually more sophisticated and more complex. And we will find out the answer only if we recognize the problem and bring our knowledge of words to bear on it.

Let me turn the case around with a couple of short quotations in which one word is left out and we have a chance to think about the effect of several different alternatives. Under what conditions might this, or that, or the other word be used? And what might the result of each be?

First, this is the opening sentence of a classic American novel of the early part of this century:

> In my younger and more vulnerable years my father
> gave me some advice that I've been turning over in my
> _____ ever since.

Although I have left out one word, we still get a pretty good idea of what the sentence is telling us: we are familiar with the expression of turning something over in the _____, and we have probably done so ourselves. A number of different words could be used to convey the general idea. Here are a few of the possibilities, listed in alphabetical order:

brain
cerebellum
head
mind
soul
spirit

They would not serve equally well, and they are not inter-
changeable, however, as each would create a slightly different
effect. Not so much in the "meaning" of the sentence as in its
power to begin shaping our understanding of what the speaker
is like and how we are to interpret what he tells us, now and
hereafter. But only the beginning of an understanding.

If the writer had put the word *cerebellum* in the mouth of the
speaker, we might instinctively think of the speaker as preten-
tious; but he might turn out to be comical, or scientific, or some
semblance of one of these. We have to wait and see. But at least
we have been given a hint that looks away from some of the other
possibilities. If he had said *soul* or *spirit*, we might feel that this
sign is a clue in the direction of loftiness or idealism; but we
would still have to see more of the context to be sure. The word
chosen is a single sign, a clue, in a pattern that is continually in
development until the text is concluded.

The word that was actually used in this text is *mind*. The book
is F. Scott Fitzgerald's *The Great Gatsby* (1925), and the speaker
is the narrator of the book (and an actor in it), Nick Carraway.
Mind is an ordinary word to use here, one that fills out a cliché
and serves as a clue in the direction of the commonplace. Maybe
a little more intellectual than the word *head*, but not much. Only
a clue that the speaker may be commonplace in his way of thinking, and only the barest beginning.

Consider, as a different kind of example, the opening sentence
of a notable book of non-fiction. It does not involve us in the
complication of a fictive speaker who is not the writer, and it
moves straight to the style of the book through the writer as
speaker. Although this book was published a generation ago, its
idiom is still clear to us today. Here it is, with a single verb left
out:

Readers of the *Odyssey* will remember the well-prepared
and touching scene in book 19, when Odysseus has at last

come home, the scene in which the old housekeeper Euryclea, who has been his nurse, _____him by a scar on
his thigh.

The situation is familiar, and the general import of the sentence is clear. The question of a fictive speaker is not at issue,
but the question of the writer (or speaker) always is. Exactly what
is he telling us? Here, in alphabetical order, is a list of various
plausible verbs that could complete the sentence:

> discerns
> fathoms
> identifies
> knows
> perceives
> recalls
> recognizes
> recollects
> remembers

The flavor of each of these verbs is a little different from the
others in this context. In the barest shorthand, I think that *discerns* would emphasize seeing through something that is obscure,
fathoms would feature solving a puzzling problem, *identifies* would
suggest proving an identity, *knows* would look toward general
cognition, *perceives* would imply penetrating vision, *recalls* would
suggest recovery of and reference to what had been forgotten,
recognizes would signify a matching of the present with the past,
recollects would intimate a bringing back of something from the
past, and *remembers* would connote being put in mind of something one knows. Of course there is much, much more to each
of these words, as everyone whose native language is English is
fully aware. *Recollects* often implies effort, for example, and *recall*
often suggests telling what has been recovered.

This is the opening sentence of Erich Auerbach's *Mimesis*
(1954); in this text, Euryclea *recognizes* Odysseus: that is, she is
struck by the awareness that this man is, by the sign of the scar,
the same person she had known before. It is not implied that
the act was difficult for her (*discerns*) or that it involved cogitation
(*fathoms*) or special vision (*perceives*) or special effort (*recollects*) or
that she had ever forgotten him (*recalls*) or that naming him was

the important thing (*identifies*); it is implied that her act was more than a sheer incident of cognition (*knows*) or of being put in mind of him (*remembers*).

I offer this example not to praise or dispraise Auerbach or the translator for this choice of words but to try to notice more fully what his text is telling us. Any of the eight other verbs might serve, perhaps, but they would give us a little different feeling about what Euryclea did.

So much by way of brief introduction to a large topic—the power of the word. I would like to offer a few examples of some of the ways that our understanding of a discourse is influenced or guided or controlled by the individual word of the text. It is very difficult to keep out of our minds all the other features that go to make up the style, like the structures of the discourse and the pattern and sound of the sentence. But I hope that we can succeed in keeping our attention, so far as possible, on the power of the word. For a similar reason, I will not include examples of strong indirect statement (like the irony of Swift's "Modest Proposal," say); it is more to our purpose to be able to go straight to the operation of the individual word in action rather than having first to sort out the way that the mode of discourse is controlling the whole passage and then see what the individual words are doing within the pattern of irony or hyperbole or whatever. I chose the examples, from Bacon and Dryden to Roosevelt and Churchill, with these needs in mind, and examples could of course be multiplied indefinitely.

First, some examples that focus on the influence of one single word on its context. Next, some ways that a few words can exert influence on a discourse and give it direction. And finally, some ways that words work together in combination and control a discourse.

I

This is the opening sentence of Winston Churchill's notable Statement to the House of Commons, delivered on October 8, 1940, in the midst of dark days for Britain:

> A month has passed since Herr Hitler turned his rage
> and malice onto the civil population of our great cities
> and particularly on London. He declared in his speech

on September 4 that he would raze our cities to the ground and since then he has been trying to carry out his _____ purpose.

The blank might have been filled by *cruel* or *wicked* or *deadly* or *fierce* or some such word that was a match for the preceding *rage* and *malice* and *raze*. But the word that Churchill actually used was *fell*. This word was obsolete in 1940, but Churchill could get away with using it within the framework of strong rhetoric. In that context, it creates a striking effect that combines the attributes of savagery and ruthlessness. The boldness of this word does a good deal to prepare the hearers for the discourse that follows, in which grave trials and tribulations are set before them as the immediate future they are to expect.

For a different kind of example, consider the Epistle Dedicatory that Francis Bacon put in front of his great multiform work, the *Magna Instauratio* (1620). His Dedication, to King James I, began as follows:

> Your Majesty may perhaps accuse me of _____, having stolen from your affairs so much time as was required for this work. I know not what to say for myself.

What word? Some modest self-deprecation, like *inattention*, or perhaps *delinquency*? Or a stronger term, like *negligence*? Not at all. Bacon's word was *larceny*. We know that such a grave charge against the self must in this context be taken as absurd or comical or redirectable. He goes on in the dedication to assert that he can't pay the King back for the time, "unless it be that what has been abstracted from your business may perhaps go to the memory of your name and the honour of your age, if these things are indeed worth anything." The audacious word *larceny* thus leads to the creation of a new kind of compliment for the King and (not entirely incidentally) to an indirect acknowledgment of the value of the book being dedicated.

The opening of Thomas Paine's *The Rights of Man* (1791) offers another example of the reflexive power of a single word:

> Among the _____ by which nations or individuals provoke and irritate each other, Mr. Burke's pamphlet on the French revolution is an extraordinary instance. Neither the people of France nor the national assembly were trou-

bling themselves about the affairs of England and the English parliament; and why Mr. Burke should commence an unprovoked attack upon them, both in parliament and in public, is a conduct that cannot be pardoned on the score of manners, nor justified on that of policy.

Would we be inclined to fill in the blank with *wrongs* or *offenses* or *misdeeds* or *transgressions*? Or some stronger word? Paine used the word *incivilities*. At first glance, this may seem like an inappropriate term to apply to Burke's *Reflections on the Revolution in France*, a masterpiece of rhetoric in defense of the old order. And yet, upon reflection, we can see that Paine has squeezed the word to make it cover a lot of ground. He has made it apply both to governmental actions and to private manners and has mingled the two. And thus the "unprovoked attack" of "Mr. Burke's pamphlet" is made to seem like a dastardly assault by a wicked man / government while maintaining the cool cover of understatement.

For one last example, consider the opening sentences of section 4 of William Blake's *Marriage of Heaven and Hell* (1790). I will leave out the familiar key term (which appears in four different forms) just so that we can think about alternate words for a moment:

Those who _____desire, do so because theirs is weak enough to be _____ed; and the _____er or reason usurps its place & governs the unwilling.

And being _____'d, it by degrees becomes passive, till it is only the shadow of desire.

Think what a difference it would make to the passage—and to much of Blake's central ideas—if he had thought *inhibit* here (with its more limited sense of psychological suppression) or *check* (bringing things under control) or *confine* (setting a permissible boundary). Blake's word was, of course, *restrain*, which suggests the use of strong force or authority to prevent or suppress or control something—in this case, the energy of desire. *Restrain* opens up, negatively, a central feature of Blake's ideas. It associates the restrainer with reason, which has the authority that the world gives it to govern people and prevent the exercise of essential human energy. *Restrain* is the key word here for Blake, and it exerts its dark power throughout the passage and throughout Blake's thought.

In the examples from Churchill and Bacon and Paine, a single word is endowed with special power because it is unusual or unexpected in the context. In the passage from Blake, the single word is unusual mainly because it accumulates much special significance and then spreads that significance throughout the context. By consequence, the power of the single word influences the impact of the discourse.

II

Sometimes a few words in a discourse can be the special clues that guide our understanding. Here is the first sentence of Part II of Thomas DeQuincey's *Confessions of an English Opium-Eater* (1821–1822), on "The Pleasures of Opium":

> It is very long since I first took opium; *so* long that, if it had been a trifling incident in my life, I might have forgotten its date: but cardinal events are not to be forgotten; and, from circumstances connected with it, I remember that this inauguration into the use of opium must be referred to the spring or to the autumn of 1804; during which seasons I was in London, having come thither for the first time since my entrance at Oxford.

We seem to be considering the simple question of a date: when did he first take opium? The guiding phrases of the passage are, I think, *trifling incident* on the one hand, and *cardinal event* on the other. The polarity of these two phrases points us to the realization—unstated and thereby the more powerful—that this *when* is not just a date. It is in fact a truly cardinal event of his life, and a fateful occasion. With that understanding, we begin to read his account of the pleasures of opium.

Or consider the effect that John Dryden creates by using a few diminishing words in the very first sentence of his Epistle Dedicatory to Lord Buckhurst, prefaced to *Of Dramatic Poesy* (1668):

> As I was lately reviewing my loose papers, amongst the rest I found this Essay, the writing which, in this rude and indigested manner wherein your Lordship now sees it,

served as an amusement to me in the country, when the violence of the last plague had driven me from the town.

The diminishing words are, I think, those *loose* papers, the *rude* and *indigested* manner, and the *amusement*. These few words serve to set the tone of the passage within the convention of self-depreciation. Dryden can then proceed merrily along and put himself forward in a chatty, informal manner. And when he gets to his address To the Reader, he can continue in his lightsome mood by referring to "this incorrect Essay, written in the country without the help of books, or advice of friends."

Sometimes a few words in a discourse can have a relatively large effect. Consider the opening of Thomas Carlyle's *Sartor Resartus* (1833–1834). The first paragraph of the "Preliminary" begins with these solemn and pompous sentiments:

> Considering our present advanced state of culture, and how the Torch of Science has now been brandished and borne about, with more or less effect, for five-thousand years and upwards; how, in these times especially, not only the Torch still burns, and perhaps more fiercely than ever, but innumerable Rush-lights, and Sulphur-matches, kindled thereat, are also glancing in every direction, so that not the smallest cranny or doghole in Nature or Art can remain unilluminated,—it might strike the reflective mind with some surprise that hitherto little or nothing of a fundamental character whether in the way of Philosophy or History, has been written on the subject of Clothes.

The language is inflated, to be sure, but within the paragraph we see the little words that begin to puncture this inflation. What were lighted at that great Torch of Science? Well, "Rush-lights, and Sulphur-matches." And what is the mark of the success of this illumination? That it lights up "the smallest cranny or doghole." It is these words that stand against the high seriousness, and thus can introduce a low topic—"Clothes"—as the subject on which to build his satire.

The beginning of Edward Gibbon's *Decline and Fall of the Roman Empire* (1776) shows another kind of alteration to the discourse from the power of a few words, this time only three. For the moment, I am leaving their places blank:

In the second century of the Christian Æra, the empire
of Rome comprehended the fairest part of the earth, and
the most civilized portion of mankind. The frontiers of
that extensive monarchy were guarded by ancient renown
and disciplined valour. The gentle, but powerful, influence of laws and manners had gradually cemented the
union of the provinces. Their peaceful inhabitants enjoyed and _____the advantages of wealth and luxury.
The image of a free constitution was preserved with __

_____

This is a smooth, harmonious, rhythmical discourse. At the
outset, everything about the Roman Empire in the second century seems deserving of praise. Consider what words might seem
apt for the blanks. What else did those peaceful inhabitants do
with their advantages of wealth and luxury besides *enjoyed* them?
used? *relished*? *exploited*? And did they preserve their free constitution with *great care*, or with *grave responsibility*, or with *supreme
veneration*?

By no means. In Gibbon's words, they *abused* their advantages,
and they preserved their constitution with *decent reverence*, no
more. These two expressions undercut the whole discourse, give
it a new flavor, and turn it in another direction.

For an even more radical example of how it would be possible
to reverse the intent of a discourse by the choice of only a couple
of substantive words, consider the following passage, with two
words left blank. It is the beginning of Addison's *Spectator*
No. 215, of November 6, 1711:

I consider an Human Soul without Education like
Marble in the Quarry, which shews none of its inherent
_____, till the Skill of the Polisher fetches out the Col-
ours, makes the Surface shine, and discovers every ____
Cloud, Spot and Vein that runs thro' the Body of it.

I expect that the natural instinct of most of us, with a built-
in bias in favor of our selves and our kind, would be to insert
favorable words in these blanks. Like "inherent *Beauties*" and
"every *ornamental* Cloud." But suppose a cynic were choosing the
words and said "inherent *Ugliness*" and "every *disfiguring* Cloud"?
The context remains relatively neutral during either of these

manipulations. The two words thus dominate the passage and create a consistent sense around these words; the context accommodates to these words. In comparison with the favorable words, the cynic's choices turn the whole discourse upside down, right on its head. Another kind of power of words.

P.S. Addison chose the favorable words.

III

The power of words often controls the whole discourse. This is most obviously and most commonly the case when words of one type are set working together; they create the tone and the attitude as well as the meaning.

It would be hard to find a clearer example than Franklin D. Roosevelt's First Inaugural Address, of March 4, 1933—the speech that Harry Hopkins considered the best that Roosevelt ever made. Remember the situation: the banks were closed, unemployment was high, business was at a standstill. The speech conveyed optimism and hope to a nation in despair. Roosevelt projected confidence—in the nation, in the people, in himself—through the power of the words of his Address.

The essence of his speech is in the very first paragraph:

> This great Nation will endure as it has endured, will revive and will prosper. So, first of all, let me assert my firm belief that the only thing we have to fear is fear itself—nameless, unreasoning, unjustified terror which paralyzes needed efforts to convert retreat into advance.

The discourse features strong, positive words:

great Nation
will endure
has endured
will revive
will prosper
firm belief
needed efforts
advance

At the same time, the discourse cites and rejects negative words:

fear
fear itself

nameless, unreasoning, unjustified terror
paralyzes
retreat

This polarity of words strengthens the positive words and tends to drive out hesitation or uncertainty. Of course the famous clause—"the only thing we have to fear is fear itself"—adds memorability to this positive way with words.

For a good example of the negative way, consider the conclusion of Henry James's *Hawthorne* (1880, in the English Men of Letters series):

> He was not a moralist, and he was not simply a poet. The moralists are weightier, denser, richer in a sense; the poets are more purely inconclusive and irresponsible. He combined in a singular degree the spontaneity of the imagination with a haunting care for moral problems. Man's conscience was his theme, but he saw it in the light of a creative fancy which added, out of its own substance, an interest, and, I may almost say, an importance.

James moves toward a meaning through a series of successive negative approximations. The underlying question seems to be: How can we get it right? How can we choose the right words? Roosevelt's address works by piling up a lot of positive words in the expectation that a meaning will evolve from these cumulative choices: it is like this and like this and like this and like this. James walks through a minefield of (to him) not quite right choices, with asides and interpolations to keep us out of trouble, in the expectation that a meaning will evolve from these near-choices: it is not just this but a little like this, not just that but a little like that, and so forth. The positive way conveys a sense of certainty about ideas and words; the negative way conveys a sense of fastidiousness in trying to choose the right words to exercise their power.

Here, for a final example of the power of words to control a whole discourse, is one in which the words are plain, ordinary, and simple. This is the beginning of Thoreau's *Walden* (1854), the first paragraph of the first chapter, entitled "Economy":

> When I wrote the following pages, or rather the bulk of them, I lived alone, in the woods, a mile from any

neighbor, in a house which I had built myself, on the shore of Walden Pond, in Concord, Massachusetts, and earned my living by the labor of my hands only. I lived there two years and two months. Now I am back living in the town.

I want to confess right away that I have revised the last little sentence of this paragraph. Although the idea is Thoreau's, the words are not. I have substituted for his words some other words that are as plain as those of the rest of his paragraph.

The words that Thoreau himself used for that last sentence were words of a different cast. He said:

At present I am a sojourner in civilized life again.

These are not the plain, ordinary, simple words of the rest of the paragraph. They have a different flavor, and the difference draws our attention to these words. The plain thought of both versions is more or less the same. But Thoreau's version conveys a message that goes beyond the plain thought. His message may be suggested in some such way as this:

At present (I don't know for how long) I am a sojourner (I feel rather like a visitor, as a matter of fact) in civilized life again (at least that's what you call it). (I don't know what my future will be like.)

At least, I think that is the effect that should be created when we perform this text. The power of the ten words in his little sentence alters the structural sense of the whole paragraph. It detaches the writer from the account of his life and opens up another way of looking at his past and at his future. And it gives a special perspective to everything that follows in the rest of its chapter, and indeed in the entire rest of the book.

6.

THE RELATION OF THE WRITER AND THE READER
The Oral Tradition

We are drawn first of all to the human side of everything. Who brought it to pass? What was he or she like? Deep thinkers sometimes get irritated at this inclination, particularly when they are driven by a wish to get on with their own discourse on the significance of the thing itself.

This impulse engages our interest in all spheres of human activity. About waging war and making peace, about noxious deeds and noble accomplishments. And about the texts of the written word, as we read them.

Drama and fiction and biography capitalize on this impulse and build their structures around the complex elements of human behavior. This includes the relations portrayed among human beings and (sometimes, perhaps often) the relation between the reader's perception of him or her self and what transpires in the text.

This impulse also affects our reading of expository prose. The sense of the writer (or speaker) and of the reader (or hearer) is often present in expository prose, and the relationship of the two has a bearing (sometimes of considerable importance, sometimes of less) on our reading of the text.

I would like to try to open up this large and important topic by looking at the tradition of oral performance that lies behind and within written prose. First—as background—something about the place of the oral tradition in the theories of rhetoric from classical antiquity through the 16th century. Then I would like to offer, with brief commentary, a few sample written texts that are in the oral tradition: several texts of orations from the 16th and 17th centuries, several texts of sermons from the 17th century to our own time, and several texts of speeches from the 19th century.

Many written texts of the past and of the present reflect the vitality and force of the oral tradition. I believe that our understanding of the style of all such texts will be enhanced if we read them with a lively awareness of the nature of the oral tradition in mind.

I

It is sometimes helpful to stumble on an inappropriate question while clambering over familiar material. Suppose we ask ourselves what relation between the writer and the reader is assumed or advised in principal works on rhetoric in classical antiquity— and take works by Plato, Aristotle, Cicero, and Quintilian as our sample. We quickly realize that this is not the question to ask. The question has to be the related one about the relation of the speaker (or orator) and his hearers (or audience).

For the essential focus of those works of rhetoric is on oratory. The most important work of Plato's for rhetoric is the *Phaedrus* (early 4th century B.C.). Its main theme is rhetoric—or rhetoric and love!—but rhetoric as applied exclusively to the art of speaking. Speaking is described as the only form of discourse that deserves to be treated seriously. In fact, toward the end of the dialogue Socrates discredits the written word as only a plaything or a method of reminding us of what we already knew, and he tells the story of the Egyptian god who denounced the inventor of letters because his invention would produce forgetfulness and the appearance of wisdom without its reality. Socrates lays great stress on the speaker knowing his audience; he maintains that a speaker can never attain perfection unless he knows the character of his hearers and adapts his discourse to them.

Aristotle's *Rhetoric* (of about 330 B.C.) is in fact his systematic treatise on public speaking, including detailed treatment of the branches of oratory, the means of persuasion, the forms of proof, and style and arrangement of speeches. He offers instruction to everyone for aid in public speaking—the primary form of communication—while forwarding truth and justice. Since the hearers determine the success of the speech, Aristotle lays special stress on them. He devotes a major part of the treatise to a discussion of how the speaker should go about creating a desirable impression of himself on his hearers while keeping in touch with them so that they will be in the right frame of mind. He refers only casually (III.12) to written prose, simply to mention that its style is different from that of spoken oratory.

Cicero's major work on rhetoric is his *De Oratore* (of about 55 B.C.). He was himself the most illustrious Roman orator, and in this dialogue on rhetoric he sought to describe the pattern of the perfect orator. He took oratory to be of supreme importance in the control of practical affairs (like the current use of "the media"), and his treatise is intended to be a guide for statesmen and other key leaders. Oratory required wide education and much practice. Cicero is at particular pains to describe (II.42–53) the way in which the speaker should present himself to his hearers, and the efforts that he should make in trying to secure the favor of his hearers. The speech is a performance before an audience, and a performance that must be entirely sincere and without trickery or make-believe. These matters touching the relation of the speaker and the hearers are second to none in importance, he maintains, in obtaining oratorical success.

Quintilian's treatise on rhetoric—called the *Institutio Oratoria* (the teaching of rhetoric), of the late 1st century A.D.—is the longest (12 solid books) and most elaborate of all the extant classical books on rhetoric. Cicero was Quintilian's great hero. For Quintilian, rhetoric was a useful art—the art of speaking well: it was, for him, an art that comprehended a major part of education from early years onward. Persuasion is central to speaking well; persuading your hearers includes moving their emotions, and moving their emotions involves revealing that your own emotions are sincerely moved (VI.2). Quintilian has relatively little to say about writing, which he regards as far less important than speaking; the use of letters is to preserve the sound of words, and words should be spelled (for example) as they are pronounced (I.7). There is in Quintilian an underlying fondness for correctness, despite his contempt for pedants and sticklers; and it is a fondness that became a preoccupation of his distant followers.

From this brief sampling, it is clear that the classical tradition of rhetoric as exemplified by these persons focused attention on the spoken word. Speech making was the valued form of discourse, and the relation of the speaker and the hearers was always recognized as a key to the success of the speech. I reiterate these facts because they lead to our recognition of the centrality of the oral tradition. These facts have often or usually been obscured by commentators on classical rhetoric who were concerned with literary criticism or literary style, and who found in classical rhetoric something to answer their needs in treating the province of the written word.

The classical tradition of rhetoric continued through the early Christian period and the Middle Ages. Dozens (or perhaps even hundreds) of treatises (mostly as commentaries on earlier works) were composed for instruction or guidance, and they carried on the classical tradition in one form or another. At the same time, the written word gradually gained more prominence as rhetoric developed. Preaching emerged as a very important form of discourse during the early Christian period, and a large body of treatises developed around its practice. The sermon is, of course, a specialized form of oratory, with a speaker and hearers, and it is responsive to the principles of classical rhetoric.

I conclude this brief look backwards into the early tradition of rhetoric with a comment on one notable 16th century English book on rhetoric, by Thomas Wilson. Called *The Arte of Rhetorique, for the use of all suche as are studious of Eloquence*, it was first published in 1553, went through at least eight editions by 1585, and was perhaps the most popular English rhetoric of its century. It continues the classical tradition of rhetoric as being focused on public speaking. The first two books are based on Quintilian, and the third (and last) also on Cicero. The orator, the types of oratory, important because they deal with weighty matters, the parts of an oration, figures and tropes. Eloquence and the need to persuade, to get the good will and move the affections of the hearers; and he who will stir the affections must first be moved himself. Composition is described as the process of joining words together so that the ear may delight in hearing the harmony. Writing is alluded to only casually, but most of the discussion of finding material and setting the style of presentation could apply as well to writing as to speaking. So it would come to be, later in the century and in the centuries that followed, as the preeminence of oratory gave way to the preeminence of the written word.

But in the latter part of the 16th century oratory was still casting a large shadow of influence over the written word. Toward the end of *The Defence of Poesie* (1581/1595), Sir Philip Sidney speaks about persuasion as an element of poetry, remarks that it is a chief feature of oratory, and then smoothly moves into some comments on oratory. He quickly catches himself, however, and says, "But what? me thinkes I deserve to be pounded, for straying from Poetrie to Oratorie; but both have such an affinity in this wordish consideration, that I think this digression, will make my meaning receive the fuller understanding."

Sidney was not alone in trying to elevate the status of poetry by transferring to it some of the high esteem in which oratory was held. William Webbe was more explicit in his "Preface to the Noble Poets of England" before his *Discourse of English Poetry* (1586); of poetry, he says, "why should we think so basely of this rather than of her sister—I mean rhetorical elocution? Which, as they were by birth twins, by kind the same, by original of one descent . . ." would argue for the equality of poetry with oratory. Puttenham gave the third chapter of his *Art of English Poesy* (1589) the resounding title, "How Poets were the First Priests, the First Prophets, the First Legislators and Politicians in the World." And Shelley was still preaching from that same gospel in his *Defence of Poetry* (1821).

In its classical tradition and at least through the 16th century, rhetoric was thought of as a way to forward truth and justice in important human affairs. Rhetoric was a principal core of secondary education, and it provided a main method for developing human expressiveness.

The tradition that lies behind rhetoric is (I say again) essentially a tradition of speechmaking. The elements are simply a speaker who wishes to persuade his hearers by a successful presentation and hearers who are at least willing to listen.

The elements are simple, but the consequences are profound. As N. Scott Momaday has his Indian preacher (his Priest of the Sun) say, in *House Made of Dawn*, "the simple act of listening is crucial to the concept of language, more crucial even than reading and writing, and language in turn is crucial to human society" (New York: Harper & Row, 1968, p. 94).

The action of the oral tradition, with a speaker and an audience, creates a basic dramatic situation that may vary from elementary to exquisitely complex. The response of the hearer affects the speaker, and the further performance of the speaker in turn modifies the response of the hearer, and so on back and forth through the entire text. In its more complex, written form, we as readers take the part of the hearers. We respond to the writer, and the illusion is sometimes created that the writer is in turn responding to us. Thus the tradition exercises its power.

We may think, from our point of view, that the oral tradition is of the distant past. We may assume that it is associated only with primitive society, when reciting (or chanting) heroic poems was in flower. But of course this is not true. The written tradition that surrounds us has grown up around the oral tradition, but certainly has not supplanted it.

We may think that written texts are entirely in the written tradition simply because they are in fact written down. But of course this is not true either. Written texts often have the features of both traditions at once. The more clearly we see the signs of the oral tradition in them, the better we can perform and understand them.

II

The classical tradition of oratory was carried on for a great many centuries in oral performance. It was also carried on in written texts, most purely in written works that take the form of orations. Although they were not intended for oral performance, they translate features of oratory to the written word. Including some sense of the relation of the writer and the reader.

Erasmus's *Praise of Folly* (1509) is a model example. It follows a form of the classical oration, with Exordium, Narration, Partition, Confirmation, and Peroration. The orator is Folly, and she steps forward to speak to the crowded assembly that is her audience—all of us readers. Her first remarks—about herself and the audience—are witty and open and almost frolicsome. This beginning is intended to put the audience in a receptive mood and to establish an easy relationship between the speaker and the audience. This is the basic requirement of the exordium of the classical oration. Erasmus fulfills it wonderfully well: he sets the tone and the relationship at once, and with great economy. The success of the entire work in good measure depends on keeping that relationship active and building on it. Needless to say, that relationship remains sharp and vivid, and the book is a great triumph.

Sir Philip Sidney's *Defence of Poesie* (1581/1595) is also in the form of a classical oration; the modern scholarly edition gives the classical terms in marginal notes to indicate where each part and sub-part begins. In the *Defence,* Sidney is himself the orator, in his own person, and he performs with gracefulness, wit, modesty, and inventiveness. He begins his exordium with the story about his going with Edward Wotton to learn horsemanship from Pugliano at the court of the Emperor Maximilian II in Vienna: Pugliano was so enamored of horses and horsemanship that he almost tried to persuade Sidney (so Sidney feels) to have wished himself a horse. So far will affection take you! So with Sidney and poetry. Having "slipped into the title of poet," he offers us his own defense of his "unelected vocation" out of affection for poetry, despite the low opinion in which (he asserts) it is held. His exordium is easy, personal, engaging, and self-disparaging—all with the light touch of jest. It follows the precedents of the classical oration in setting up a relation between the speaker and the audience: even as readers we are made to feel that we are in fact the audience for this seemingly spontaneous performance going on in front of us. The relationship continues through the rest of the *Defence* as we seem to be the hearers of a pleasant, intelligent, thoughtful discourse.

John Milton's *Areopagitica* (1644) is such a good example of a classical oration that it is sometimes given to students of oratory for analysis. "I wrote *Areopagitica,*" Milton said later, in his *Second Defence,* "according to the model of a regular speech," and it was entitled *Areopagitica: A Speech of Mr. John Milton For the Liberty of Unlicenc'd Printing, To the Parlament of England.* Of course Milton never expected to deliver it as a speech, but he availed himself of the form in order to gain the effects of oratory. The discourse is in the first person of "I" and "We," and the audience (reader) is always addressed as "You." The exordium (several pages in length) presents the orator as a high-minded idealist—one who feels obliged to speak out on this occasion because of his passionate love of liberty. The audience (Members of Parliament/ readers) is figured as a body of prudent, wise, brave people. The entire speech is full of learning and allusion, and it stays one complete step ahead of the reader in anticipating and answering objections that might be raised. Its rather aloof manner makes it appealing only to a relatively limited group of readers, perhaps, and it offers few concessions for broadening that audience in (for example) the ways of jest and self-disparagement that

Erasmus and Sidney thought fit to use. It gives the impression of solidity and rightness in its argument and in its logic. Some of its attractiveness comes from its idealism, and some from the feeling of involvement created by the explicit relation of the speaker and the audience. The speaker is learned and cultivated, and he is a true lover of liberty. We are treated as if we too are learned and cultivated and true lovers of liberty. It is a pleasing role to be given, even if not much human warmth comes along with it.

The appeal of each of these three texts derives in some measure from our sense of the relation of the speaker and the audience. Our sense of this relation involves us personally in a dramatic situation, and that involvement is important to the way we read and perform and understand the text.

III

For many centuries, from the early Middle Ages onward, sermons reached a far larger audience than any other type of non-ritualistic discourse, whether oral or written. They are entirely in the oral tradition, of course, with the sermonist as the speaker and the congregation as the hearers, and with a live relation possible between the two. The sermon gains in potential effect because of the hallowed nature of the occasion and the religious nature of the message. Moreover, the speaker is a figure endowed with special authority and set apart from the willing hearers who are listening.

Reading the written text of a sermon is a somewhat different experience from hearing it performed, of course. Jeremy Taylor thought that, ideally, both experiences would be engaging; "it is fit," he wrote in the dedication to his *XXVII Sermons* (1668), "that men should be affected and employed when they hear and read sermons." The translation from oral to written form has sometimes caused misgivings for the sermonist, however. Martin Luther King, Jr., for example, wrote in the Preface to his sermons collected under the title *Strength to Love* (1963):

> I have been rather reluctant to have a volume of sermons printed. My misgivings have grown out of the fact that a sermon is not an essay to be read but a discourse to be heard. It should be a convincing appeal to a listening con-

gregation. Therefore, a sermon is directed toward the listening ear rather than the reading eye. While I have tried to rewrite these sermons for the eye, I am convinced that this venture could never be entirely successful. So even as this volume goes to press I have not altogether overcome my misgivings.

All true. The translation may "never be entirely successful" because the power of the oral tradition is usually strong enough to resist extirpation and to endow the written text with at least some of its special kind of power.

I would like to offer sample opening passages from the written texts of several sermons in order to observe some ways in which a relation is established between the writer and the reader. One way is direct address. Here is the beginning of Hugh Latimer's great Convocation Sermon of 1536:

> Brethren, ye be come together this day, as far as I perceive, to hear of great and weighty matters. Ye be come together to entreat of things that most appertain to the commonwealth. This being thus, ye look, I am assured, to hear of me—which am commanded to make as a preface this exhortation, albeit I am unlearned and unworthy—such things as shall be much meet for this your assembly. I therefore, not only very desirous to obey the commandment of our Primate but also right greatly coveting to serve and satisfy all your expectations, lo, briefly and as plain as I can, will speak of matters both worthy to be heard in your congregation and also of such as best shall become mine office in this place.

The form of direct address makes an appeal to the audience and serves as a kind of exordium. The speaker is also projecting an image of himself—in this case, a self-diminished image—along with a feeling of respect for the members of the audience. The warning of plainness was, in fact, preparation for an attack on the listeners. Latimer went on to condemn the abuses of the higher clergy and to accuse the very audience before him of incompetence and corruption.

Most sermons are more amiable. Here is the way that Lancelot Andrewes sets the relationship with his audience in his Christmas sermon preached before the King at Whitehall in 1605, on the text "For verily he took not on him the nature of angels, but he took on him the seed of Abraham" (Hebrews ii.16):

> And, even because, this *day,* He tooke not the *Angells* upon Him, but took our Nature, in the *seede* of *Abraham*; therefore hold wee this *Day,* as a high *Feast*: therefore meet we thus, every yeare, in a holy Assembly; even, as for a solemne *memorial,* that He hath, as this day, bestowed upon us a dignity, which upon the *Angells,* He bestowed not.

The balancing use of "He" and "We" pairs God and Man, of course. But the pairing and the "We" also associate the speaker and the audience in a common enquiry, and the relation quickly and quietly brings us all together in a joint activity. The impression is created that the speaker is exploring the question along with the rest of us and for our mutual benefit. Andrewes continues this attitude through the sermon. The relation of speaker and reader (as suggested by these few following lines from the conclusion of this sermon) may account in part for the special attraction that Andrewes had for readers of recently past times, like T. S. Eliot:

> It is most kindly, to take part with Him, in that, which He tooke part in, with us; and that, to no other end, but that He might make the *receiving* of it by us, a meanes, whereby He might *dwell in us, and we in Him.* He *taking our flesh,* and we *receiving* His *spirit*; by His *flesh,* which He *took of us, receiving* His *spirit,* which He imparteth to us.

Thus, in the end, "We" and "Us" have been given a corporate identity that unifies, unites the speaker (writer) and the listener (reader).

Many sermons are less amiable and yet effective in establishing a relation between writer and reader. Let me offer, as one example of a Puritan sermon, Cotton Mather's "The Saviour with his Rainbow" (1714). Underlying this and similar sermons are some assumptions (such as the sinfulness of the audience, the extreme need for aid, and the special role of the speaker) that help to direct the relation between speaker and hearers. This is the opening paragraph of Mather's sermon:

> It is the *Head* of your admirable Saviour, which, O dis-

tressed People of God, now appears before you. Oh! behold it, with sweet Encouragements; with just Astonishments! The *Head* about which we now see the comfortable *Rainbow,* is *thy Head,* O thou Church of the Living God; it is he, whom God has placed as *thy Head,* and thou thy self hast chosen him, hast owned him.

Mather's sermon is full of zeal and exhortation. He enjoins his hearers/readers to look up and imagine a scene which he describes, then to place themselves personally in that scene. Later he says, "My Friend, apply the glorious rainbow to thy own *particular Condition*; thy Saviour invites thee to do so." The rainbow is a sign of God's covenant with the living Church, but it is also a reminder of the need for individual repentance, the need to appease an angry God. The "sweet Encouragments" turn out to be the assurance that appeasement is possible, through repentance.

It is hard to say what kind of relation was initially established between a speaker (writer) and listener (reader) in a given case without knowing a good deal about the speaker, the listeners, the situation, and actual reactions of the listeners. For many of the most popular preachers (John Wesley, for example), there is a wealth of recollections of the sermons, and from them one can gain a sense of the range of the reactions.

It is relatively easy for us to record our own sense of the relation as it strikes us as readers. Many people today would say that the beginning of Mather's sermon is absurd, and they would turn away from the invitation to a relationship. Every written record is ultimately subject to a judgment that disregards its history. Part of the success of any discourse in the oral tradition depends on forming a sympathetic (or at least workable) relation between the speaker and the hearer, and this is the job of the speaker. We know that the hearers of Cotton Mather's sermons were, in general, mightily impressed by them, despite their severity and the underlying assumption of the speaker's special relation with God. And we can infer that the speaker's strategy for establishing an effective relation with his own audience was quite successful. We are entirely free, of course, to join in that relation, or to turn away.

The relation between John Henry Newman and his audience

was built on a sense of calm and peace. Here is the opening of his sermon on "The Invisible World" (2 Corinthians iv.18), delivered while he was still a clergyman of the Church of England:

There are two worlds, 'the visible and the invisible', as the Creed speaks,—the world we see, and the world we do not see; and the world which we do not see as really exists as the world we do see. It really exists though we see it not. The world that we see we know to exist, because we see it. We have but to lift up our eyes and look around us, and we have proof of it: our eyes tell us. We see the sun, moon and stars, earth and sky, hills and valleys, woods and plains, seas and rivers. And again, we see men, and the works of men. We see cities, and stately buildings, and their inhabitants; men running to and fro, and busying themselves to provide for themselves and their families, or to accomplish great designs, or for the very business' sake.

And he continues in this vein, piling up certainties around us. Immediately we sense an attitude of trust in us. "We" are important. What "we" do matters. What "we" see is what is there. It is on this sense of relation that Newman builds his sermon. As he approaches his conclusion, he can say:

We may increase indeed for ever in knowledge and in love, still that first waking from the dead, the day at once of our birth and our espousals, will ever be endeared and hallowed in our thoughts. When we find ourselves after long rest gifted with fresh powers, vigorous with the seed of eternal life within us, able to love God as we wish, conscious that all trouble, sorrow, pain, anxiety, bereavement, is over for ever, blessed in the full affection of those earthly friends whom we loved so poorly, and could protect so feebly, while they were with us in the flesh. . . .

The speaker appears to assume that he is in close touch with the audience and that we believe what he has to say. He tells us about ourselves, our experiences, and our sentiments. He feels able to tell us about our future and how we will react to it. The main strategy of this kind of text is establishing an easy relation with the audience and building on that foundation.

For a final example of a sermon, I would like to quote the opening of one of the sermons that Martin Luther King, Jr. wrote while in jail in Georgia about 1960 and that he delivered during and after the bus protests in Montgomery, Alabama. This one is entitled "Shattered Dreams" (printed in *Strength to Love,* 1963) to the text of St. Paul's words that "Whensoever I take my journey into Spain, I will come to you" (Romans xv.24). Here is King's first paragraph:

> One of the most agonizing problems within our human experience is that few, if any, of us live to see our fondest hopes fulfilled. The hopes of our childhood and the promises of our mature years are unfinished symphonies. In a famous painting, George Frederic Watts portrays Hope as a tranquil figure who, seated atop our planet, her head sadly bowed, plucks a single unbroken harpstring. Is there any one of us who has not faced the agony of blasted hopes and shattered dreams?

Thus the exordium. We all have the same agonizing experience of unfulfilled hopes, says the preacher. We are all together in the same boat. "Is there any one of us who has not faced the agony of blasted hopes and shattered dreams?" The rhetorical question can work wonders in drawing us together if we are sympathetic. No, we answer on behalf of ourselves, and we look around at others, who are also answering No. As for St. Paul, he also is answering No: he never got to Spain. On the foundation of this relation, the sermonist can propose and reject three possible human reactions before offering us an answer that we can enthusiastically accept.

In each of these sermons, features of the oral tradition are adapted to the written text in order to establish a relation between the speaker and the hearer. The form of the direct address in Latimer, the sense of engaging in a joint activity in Andrewes, the severe exhortations in Mather, the feelings of mutual trust in Newman, and the rhetorical question in King. The strategies are in fact limitless. What matters is the success in establishing a relation in which to create the structure of a discourse that will involve us as hearers or as readers.

IV

The oral tradition includes, in its central repertory, the whole world of speeches and speechmaking. Addresses or lectures they may sometimes be, or sometimes even harangues or declamations. Many of the discourses within the family of speeches have been printed, and many written texts—more, I think, than we generally realize—derive from speeches and thus from the oral tradition. We can read them better if we recognize their underlying oral form, and the way that they represent the relation between the writer and the reader.

Let us consider the situation with some 19th century texts of importance. First, a few words about the prevalence of lectures, a little about several notable practitioners, and then more attention to one single lecturer of renown, Ralph Waldo Emerson.

Public lectures became a really popular form of activity early in the 19th century, first in Britain, then in the United States, as part of a growing desire for self-education. Many institutions (Lamb said there were "ten thousand" in London) sponsored lecture series. They ranged in type from the Royal Academy to the Crown and Anchor Tavern in the Strand. A series of eight or ten lectures would be announced as covering a large general topic, such as English philosophy, or Elizabethan drama. Reasonably well-known persons got good payment for their efforts: Coleridge received 100 guineas for a series in 1808, and Thomas Campbell 100 guineas for his very first series, in 1811. Those who were less well-known often worked by subscription, inducing their friends to sell tickets for them.

Lectures were popular with the audience for the supposed educational return and with the speakers for the undoubted financial return. Printed prospectuses were put out, the rooms were often or usually crowded, and the lectures were frequently written up in newspaper reports and in private diaries. Not all of the lecturers were experienced or skillful: Hazlitt was so nervous during one of his first performances that he bolted from the platform and had to be forced back by friends before he would continue. And not all reactions were favorable: Coleridge was described as speaking in a monotone and having unclean stockings and uncombed hair. But the general reaction recorded about most lecturers tended to be one of respect, or of awe.

In the United States, the Lyceum movement provided a variety of educational experiences (including lectures) for the public, beginning in the 1820s and continuing through the century. Popular speakers or celebrities (like Charles Dickens and Matthew Arnold and Mark Twain) went on extended lecture tours, taking culture to the remote recesses of our nation. Even the later Chautauqua movement included speeches in its spectrum of popular entertainment.

Of the writers of the early 19th century whose work we value highly, Coleridge was probably the one who lectured most extensively. He began his career as a lecturer in 1795, when he was 22, within a month or two after leaving Cambridge. For more than a decade of the most active portion of his life so far as literary studies are concerned, from 1808 to 1819, lecturing was a principal occupation for him and a main source of support. More important for us, his lectures lie behind much of the prose that constitutes his written texts.

Consider his Shakespearean criticism, often described as one of the great glories of practical criticism in English. He never published it, nor prepared it for publication. He delivered it as lectures, in several series, from 1808 to 1819. What we possess is his notes on individual plays, marginalia, lecture notes and fragments, and a lot of detailed reports on his lectures as reported by J. Payne Collier, Crabb Robinson, a reporter for the *Bristol Gazette*, and J. Tomalin. In this fashion has the substance of Coleridge's Shakespearean criticism been transmitted to posterity.

Even the *Biographic Literaria* (a classic of literature and a landmark of literary criticism) is, in manner, very much like a series of speeches, even though it is not so regarded. A fact of key importance is that Coleridge *dictated* it to an amanuensis during three and a half months of the summer of 1815—which was in the middle of his most intensive period of lecturing. It has the tone and style of a speech, and its appeal and its charm are closely related to its oratorical condition.

William Hazlitt is a similar example. Most of his important literary criticism was based on lectures that he gave. Twenty-four lectures, for example, went into his three books on Elizabethan dramatic literature, English comic writers, and the English poets. He described his principle of presentation as follows: "I conceive that what I have undertaken to do in this and former cases, is merely to read over a set of authors with the audience, as I would do with a friend, to point out a favourite passage, to explain an objection; or if a remark or a theory occurs, to state it in illustration of the subject" (*Works*, ed. P. P. Howe, London, VI, 1931, 301). Hazlitt sees the relation of writer and reader as that of friends—his task is to "read over a set of authors with the audience, as I would do with a friend."

For one more similar example, John Ruskin. More than a dozen of his books were collections of his lectures. *Sesame and Lilies*, for instance, was made up of two lectures on reading in the first edition and three lectures in the second. ("I want you to feel, with me," he wrote to the reader near the beginning of Lecture II, "that whatever advantages we possess in the present day in the diffusion of education and of literature, can only be rightly used by any of us when we have apprehended clearly what education is to lead to, and literature to teach.") *The Crown of Wild Olive* comprised three lectures. Similarly, lectures on painting, architecture, wood and metal engraving, social conditions, even Greek and English birds became books of his essays. And through them all runs, for us as readers, an idea of the writer who is addressing us as his specific audience.

Coleridge and Hazlitt and Ruskin lectured a lot, but lecturing was the main occupation of Ralph Waldo Emerson for nearly fifty years. He began his career as a lecturer in 1833, when he was 30, about a year after he had resigned the pastorate of the Second Church in Boston. He turned to lecturing to support himself and his family. He had had, as preparation, the usual four years of Declamations and Forensic Debates at Harvard, and about six years of preaching sermons as a licensed minister, including three years at the Second Church. His last lecture was given in 1881, the year before his death. In between, he gave lectures first in the Boston area, then in New England and the Middle Atlantic states, then in the Midwest, California, and England. He gave a hundred lectures at the Concord Lyceum alone. In Boston, he gave many series—like ten weekly lectures on "Human Culture," with an average of 400 in attendance. He varied his topics endlessly both at home and out on the lecture circuit.

For our purposes, the crucial aspect of Emerson's lectures is that they were a basis for ALL of his books in prose, from *Nature* in 1836 to *Letters and Social Aims* in 1876 to posthumously published essays. I would like for us to sample a couple of Emerson's essays to see the ways in which they do in fact resemble speeches in establishing a relation between the writer and the reader.

Consider "The American Scholar." After delivery as the Phi Beta Kappa Address at Harvard on August 31, 1837, it was printed with little or no revision about three weeks later. It is, perhaps, the most read and most venerated of Emerson's essays, and I believe that it is now commonly thought of as a piece of expository prose, as an essay.

It begins with a long paragraph of direct address to his audience, in which the speaker joins himself and his audience together in shared experience: "our anniversary . . . our cotemporaries . . . our holiday . . . our day of dependence, our long apprenticeship to the learning of other lands." The sense of shared experience permeates the essay.

Once in a while the writer has a moment of uncertainty about his audience. Once, in self-doubt, he says, "I might not carry with me the feeling of my audience in stating my own belief" (*Collected Works*, Harvard, I, 1971, 65). But he is able to brush away the doubt. Earlier in the essay, he had put and answered the doubt in a more general situation:

> The orator distrusts at first the fitness of his frank confessions,—his want of knowledge of the persons he addresses,—until he finds that he is the complement of his hearers;—that they drink his words because he fulfills for them their own nature; the deeper he dives into his privatest secretest presentiment,—to his wonder he finds, this is the most acceptable, most public, and universally true. The people delight in it; the better part of every man feels, This is my music: this is myself. (p. 63)

The joy of this discovery is the awareness of universal harmony, but (on a mundane level) it is the relief that the speaker feels when he finds himself in tune with his audience, and his audience in tune with him. It is the most comfortable relation for ideal performance.

Oliver Wendell Holmes, who heard the speech, said that "No listener ever forgot that Address, and among all the noble utterances of the speaker it may be questioned if one ever contained more truth in language more like that of immediate inspiration." Hearing Emerson deliver his speeches created a special effect, of course. Annie Fields, after quoting from memory long passages that she remembered from hearing Emerson's lectures, said: "All this seems like a wretched prose translation of what Mr. Emerson said. The lectures themselves are poetry and music." On the other side of the water, Thomas Carlyle did *not* hear "The American Scholar." But when he read the pamphlet that contained it, he said that "I could have *wept* to read that speech; the clear high melody of it went tingling through my heart" (*Ralph Waldo Emerson,* ed. Carl Bode, New York: Hill and Wang, 1968, pp. 55, 85, 56). The point is this: hearing "The American Scholar" and reading it created similar reactions, at least for Holmes and Carlyle. In that sense, the speech and the essay are as one, and it rides on the power of the oral tradition.

For an essay of Emerson's that is much further removed from the rostrum, consider "Circles" (*Essays: First Series,* 1841; *Collected Works,* II, 1979, 179–90). It contains material that he had used and re-used in lectures on "Human Culture." But more of it is "new"—that is, sentences and passages that he took from here and there in his journals (his "savings bank," he called them) with newly written introductions and transitions. (This was, in fact, Emerson's usual way of converting a lecture into an essay— the "tinkering arts," he said—though usually he took more material from his lectures than he did in "Circles.")

The relationship of the writer and the reader is epitomized in "Circles" by one basic tactic: a continuing emphasis on "I," "We," and "You," and on the connections between them. In this essay of less than twelve pages in the *Collected Works,* "We" (our, ours, us) appears 80 times, "I" (me, mine) over 60 times, and "You" (thou, thee) about 20 times; one or another of them is used an average of 14 times per page. On the other hand, third person pronouns ("he" and "they" in particular) often suggest an outsider or a faintly distasteful situation, except when they are representing the deity.

Emerson emphasizes the relationship between the writer and the reader by frequently shifting the discourse back and forth between them. Now it is the "I" of the writer who is telling about himself, now it is the "We" of the readers and our involvement with the writer. Emerson reveals his inner thoughts to the reader, and the reader reveals his thoughts to Emerson.

I believe that an examination of most of Emerson's essays will reveal that they rely on the oral tradition in order to create their effect, and that the establishment of a relation between the writer and the reader is central to that effect. And Emerson is, for our purposes, representing a host of writers of the 19th century whose texts are based on lectures or who otherwise display some of the style of oral discourse.

V

The oral tradition humanizes the text in the sense that we are aware that the discourse is between human beings. It opens up the potentiality of a dramatic situation in which we encounter one another and begin to parley.

Sometimes that dramatic situation is realized in a vital, life-giving way. As when we are made aware of the nature of the writer and the nature of the role in which we as readers have been cast. And when the persuasive force of the relationship leads us to accept what is set forth, or to argue with it, or to reject it. Some readers may, on occasion, turn away from the role that is offered them: in that case, the discourse has failed in the oral tradition, and the text has to take its chances in the written tradition.

The oral tradition has, once again, become increasingly powerful in the course of the 20th century through the use of electronic media. The oral tradition, coupled with a visual orientation, has come to dominate popular culture. The reflective influence of this dominance has a potent impact on all the other forms of culture in which the written text had for these five centuries or so held the place of preference.

The oral tradition is, I believe, more pervasive in written texts than we commonly recognize. It is certainly not limited to the kinds of examples I have offered, orations and sermons and speeches. Most of the features that we have been noticing can be found, here and there, in one way or another, throughout the entire range of English prose.

If we seek the existence of the oral tradition in texts in which we had not perceived the hidden drama, we will perhaps be able to realize the style of the text more fully in our performance of it.

7.

THE RELATION OF THE WRITER AND THE READER
The Personal Written Tradition

Dear Abby: Can I wear a formal white gown at my wedding even though my fiancé and I have been living together these last two years? . . . How can I discourage my wife's parents from spending their vacation with us every year and still not hurt anybody's feelings? . . . Should I tell my parents that my older brother often sneaks out of the house at night after they have gone to bed?

Letters, letters, letters. "Dear Abby" is published worldwide in more than a thousand newspapers that reach some eighty million households daily. And "Dear Abby" is only one of hundreds of columns of letters and answers on diverse topics. On garden care, etiquette, coins and stamps, locating unusual items of clothing, problems with defective merchandise, investing, cooking, health, and (it seems) almost every topic that causes problems for people. Most of all, questions that treat problems we face in determining acceptable human behavior in our relations with other people.

These letters are widely read. And the readership includes people who are not troubled by the specific problems under discussion. Editors of newspapers, magazines, and even learned journals and specialized newsletters apparently realize that the letters they publish from readers are of as much interest to their subscribers as the regular content of their periodicals. From the readers' point of view, the interest is sometimes or often greater. The response does not always depend on the importance of the subject or its relevance to our private concerns; in Britain, letters reporting the hearing of the first cuckoo in spring were eagerly followed each year and ultimately became such a byword as to provide the title for a book of letters to the editor, and then another.

Why do printed letters command such interest? In many (or

most) cases, they seem more interesting and engaging—and hence more likely to be read—than would the same material cast in essay form. Why is this? I think: because they are human and specific and personal. But also: by engaging ourselves with the letters as readers of them, we complete the relation of the writer and the reader and form a human link. Thus we involve ourselves in an interpersonal activity a little like a conversation, but with freedom to begin and terminate it at our convenience, with no hard feelings.

We sometimes know who the writer and the recipient are. If not, the content of the letter generally tells us a lot about the writer and (by inference, at least) about the recipient. A letter is a human document, and we perceive it as a communication between living human beings. By its nature, the letter sets up some kind of a relation between the writer and the reader.

In the case of printed letters, as readers we often cast ourselves in the place of the recipient as if it were written to us, thus making the relation more personal than it may seem to be on the surface. We might even feel like disputing with the writer. I believe that many readers of "Dear Abby" contrive their own answers to the questions and compare their responses with the "official" answers given by Abby. Since we are the sole judge of the comparative merits of the two answers, it is not surprising if the advantage often comes our way and makes us feel better about ourselves.

I would like for us to consider the subject of the written tradition that lies behind the relation of the writer and the reader when that relation creates an effect that seems personal, or at least semi-personal. In classical antiquity, the form of prose that stood next after the oration in esteem was the letter. So let us begin by reviewing the early role of the letter as literary art, from the time of classical antiquity to the beginning of the 16th century. This is one tradition of English prose writing that is, I think, generally overlooked or misunderstood. Next, I would like for us to consider some more modern examples of the letter as a literary form. Then, to look at the way the letter functions in an auxiliary role, as in prefatory letters to a text. Finally, to look at a few examples of how some other semi-personal forms of prose (such as the dialogue, the autobiography, and the personal essay) tend to remove some of the distance between the writer and the reader, to bring the reader into the text, and to set a style.

I

The thousands of extant letters from Greek and Roman antiquity are a rich storehouse of information about the acts, observations, attitudes, and feelings of many of the most notable persons and of the history of their times. For Cicero, for example, his secretary Tiro preserved 426 *Letters to his Friends* (three Loeb Classical Library volumes); his long and elaborate "Letters to Atticus," in sixteen books, fill three more Loeb volumes; and there are two books of letters to Quintus and two books of letters to Brutus. From the Greek world, there are collections of letters by Isocrates, Plato, Plutarch, and Epicurus. From the Roman world, letters by Cato the Elder, Caesar, Seneca, and the younger Pliny. And many, many others.

These letters are a storehouse of information. But they are, as well, a form of literature. They cover a wide range of types. Some are formal, like the didactic letters of Cato to his son. Some are informal, dealing with transient topics. Whatever the type, most of the letters that have been preserved were written and sent and read as creations of literary art. And so they were regarded by later readers for many centuries.

Cicero's letters served as a primary model for some 1500 years, and the *Letters to his Friends* were a central text. His letters were often intensely personal. The letter of 54 B.C. to Publius Lentulus Spinther (Book I, ix), for example, gives a detailed account of Cicero's motives and his reasons for acting as he had done; it is like being invited to listen to a conversation that continues to be private even though it has been made public by our presence. Cicero's final thoughts on ethics are embodied in his treatise on moral duties, called *De Officiis*. Its form, however, is that of a letter to his son Marcus. In it, we come to know a good deal about the elderly, distinguished, self-satisfied writer and something of the foibles of the twenty-one year old son. This human context gives added life to the substance of the treatise, the ways of thinking about duty, and the whole moral basis of human behavior.

For another example of a slightly different kind, Seneca's essays, like "On Learning Wisdom in Old Age," "On Drunkenness," "On Practising What You Preach," and all the rest of the 124 (in three Loeb volumes). They are all in the form of letters, all written to his friend Lucilius, *Ad Lucilium Epistulae Morales.* There is enough of the sense of the letter about them to keep us reminded, by their form and their personal manner, of the human context of the writer and the reader and the importance of their interaction. As a result, we can read them with a warmth of feeling that ordinary essays usually do not generate.

Many (or perhaps most) of the letters to which I have referred were written not only for the recipient but also with a public audience in mind. The younger Pliny's principal letters, preserved in ten books (two Loeb volumes), can stand as an example. As far as the first nine books go, Pliny composed them with the expectation of publication, and in fact published them during his lifetime; only the tenth book, his official correspondence with the Emperor Trajan, was published after Pliny's death.

Letters and orations had a good deal in common, at least so far as the matter we have under discussion is concerned. The same elements of speaker/writer and hearer/reader are involved, and a similar dramatic situation is evident. It was left for the witty and willful Welshman, James Howell, to draw, on behalf of the ancients, the practical distinction between their orations and their letters. He drew it, *in a letter,* of July 25, 1625 to "Sir J. S., at Leeds Castle":

> Sir, It was a quaint Difference the ancients did put 'twixt a *Letter* and an *Oration*: that the one should be attired like a Woman, the other like a Man: the latter of the two [the oration] is allowed large side Robes, as long Periods, Parentheses, Similes, Examples, and other Parts of Rhetorical Flourishes: But a *Letter* or *Epistle* should be short-coated and closely couched; a Hungerlin [short coat] becomes a *Letter* more handsomely than a Gown: Indeed we should write as we speak; and that's a true familiar Letter which expresseth one's Mind, as if he were discoursing with the Party to whom he writes, in succinct and short Terms. The *Tongue,* and the *Pen,* are both of them Interpreters of the Mind; but I hold the Pen to be the more faithful of the two. (*Epistolae Ho-Elianae,* 1645, I, i)

From Howell's remarks, one is of course drawn to the conclusion that, in his view, the letter and the oration are fundamentally alike. The difference lies in the manner in which they are dressed. Howell takes the Modern (as opposed to the Ancient) view in preferring the letter (the pen) to the oration (the tongue) as the more faithful interpreter of the mind.

The tradition of the letter continued strong during the early Christian period. We must remind ourselves that of the twenty-seven canonical books of the New Testament, twenty-one of them are in the form of letters, or epistles. St. Paul, whose name is attached to fourteen of them, must be accounted a letter writer of the first importance. And so, among the Fathers of the Church, must be St. Jerome (154 of whose letters survive) and St. Augustine (with 276 extant letters). Gregory the Great, the 7th-century pope, was also a very influential letter writer; 850 of his letters remain with us. After a long period during which education declined, there was a modest return of interest in the letter during the 11th and 12th centuries, with several important treatises on the subject written in Bologna, Orléans, and elsewhere.

But the great resurgence in the tradition of the letter occurred during the Renaissance. Of Aretino's letters, 3,300 are extant, 495 by Michelangelo, 437 by St. Teresa of Avila, 236 by Ficino, and so forth. By the 16th century, anthologies of letters became popular, beginning with one put together by Aretino in 1537, his *Florilegium*; Montaigne was not exaggerating much when he said that a hundred more anthologies of letters appeared in the next fifty years. Later in the 16th century, they began to appear in England, at first mostly translated or adapted from the Italian. Manuals of letter writing and books of sample letters also became popular; more than sixty have been recorded in England in the 16th and 17th centuries, many of them going through several editions.

I would like to single out just one notable and influential letter writer of the Renaissance. He will have to stand for a multitude of other writers of his time, in representing the tradition of the letter.

Erasmus (1469?–1536) was probably held in higher esteem by his contemporaries for his learning than any other scholar has ever been, before or since. His contemporaries knew him as the translator of the New Testament into Latin, the editor of the correspondence of St. Jerome, the teacher of the *Colloquies*, the satirist of the *Praise of Folly*, the compiler of the *Adages*, and the scholarly author of the *Enchiridion* and a hundred other theological treatises. But the general intellectual world of his time probably valued him most of all because of his letters.

Erasmus's learned world of western Europe was united in its common language of Latin, and letters served as the prime source of news and opinion on matters of importance, in lieu of magazines and learned journals. Erasmus was a true international figure; though he called himself Erasmus of Rotterdam, he might have been known as Erasmus of Paris, Basel, Cambridge, Rome, Louvain, Antwerp, and a dozen other centers where he taught, studied, or lived. Like St. Paul, however, he never went to Spain.

Erasmus had a large circle of friends, colleagues, and potential patrons, spread all over western Europe. They included Henry VIII, Pope Leo X, and Sir Thomas More, as well as Pieter Gillis, Ulrich von Hutten, and Beatus Rhenanus. Letters from Erasmus were (like most letters of his time) shared by the recipient with others, sometimes with many others, and some were copied and passed around. It became a mark of special distinction to possess a letter from Erasmus, and many people wrote him in hopes of an answer. In his later years he said that he spent half of his day reading letters and writing them, as many as sixty to ninety a day he claimed. Only about 1,600 of his letters have survived, however, with an annual maximum of a little more than a hundred in the most prolific years of his long writing career.

He came to expect that selections of his letters would be printed, but he objected when other people collected, selected, and printed them. So he arranged to publish various collections of his own letters, and for the last twenty years of his life a collection of his letters (or a new edition of them) came out nearly every year. These publications were mainly occasioned by the clamoring demands of printers, who had a large and ready market for Erasmus's letters. In at least one case, he sent to the printer a copy of a letter even before it had gotten to the addressee (Wolfgang Capito, February 26, 1517); it is indeed an interesting letter, a splendid statement of the ideals of humanistic reform, and good for all of us to read.

There was plenty of precedent among the classical authors (including Cicero) to publish your own letters. Petrarch and others had done it in modern times. And in the immediate past, the renowned head of the Platonic Academy in Florence, Marsilio Ficino, began to collect his own letters in the 1470s, arranged them in twelve books (on the model of the *Aeneid*), circulated them in manuscript, and then had them printed in 1475.

Erasmus regarded letters as a conscious form of art, and his contemporaries generally shared this view. He wrote a treatise on the art of letter writing, called *De Conscribendis Epistolis,* in which he made the letter parallel with the classical oration, both in the types of letters/orations that might be written, and in the parts in which letters/orations might be constructed. The oral and the written traditions were thus still close at the beginning of the 16th century. Erasmus thought the letter a versatile form—he certainly used it so—with the requirement that its form be appropriate to its subject. Yet for him the letter was not to be a treatise or a declamation, but a reflection of the real life of men, like a conversation between friends. But still a form of art, public and permanent.

Let me offer, as a single example, one short passage from a letter by Erasmus to Martin Luther, who shared the world's esteem for Erasmus as a man of learning and had written to him, saying, "For who is there in whose heart Erasmus does not occupy a central place, to whom Erasmus is not the teacher who holds him in thrall? I speak of those who love learning as it should be loved. For I am not sorry if among Christ's other gifts this too finds its place, that many disapprove of you" (March 28, 1519). Many did disapprove of Erasmus the Christian humanist, as many more were to disapprove of Luther the Protestant reformer.

Here is the first paragraph of a letter of May 30, 1519 to Luther from Erasmus, who was then at the University of Louvain and observing the intellectual turmoil there as well as elsewhere:

> Greetings, dearest brother in Christ. Your letter gave me
> great pleasure: it displayed the brilliance of your mind

and breathed the spirit of a Christian. No words of mine could describe the storm raised here by your books. Even now it is impossible to root out from men's minds the most groundless suspicion that your work is written with assistance from me and that I am, as they call it, a standard-bearer of this new movement. They supposed that this gave them an opening to suppress both humane studies—for which they have a burning hatred, as likely to stand in the way of her majesty queen Theology, whom they value much more than they do Christ—and myself at the same time, under the impression that I contribute something of importance towards this outburst of zeal. In the whole business their weapons are clamour, audacity, subterfuge, misinterpretation, innuendo; if I had not seen it with my own eyes—felt it, rather—I would never have believed theologians could be such maniacs. One would think it was some disastrous infection. And yet this poisonous virus, starting in a small circle, spread to a larger number, so that a great part of this university was carried away by the spreading contagion of this epidemic paranoia. (*Collected Works*, VI, Toronto, 1982, 391–92.)

We tend to think of the letter as an entirely private communication of one person to another. That was certainly not the case from classical antiquity to the 16th century. In the tradition established during that time, the letter is a form of literary art, and it is the written parallel of a spoken speech. Its special effect derives from the relation of the writer and the reader that it establishes, and that effect carries over into its public mode as a work of art. Thus the letter becomes a basis for the tradition in the written record of the relation of the writer and the reader.

II

In English, the letter has continued to be a prominent literary form, and it has continued to dramatize the relation of the writer and the reader. The classical tradition has been carried on in a great variety of different ways, and the total effect on the structure of prose is impressive.

Let me allude to a few examples, from different times, in which the letter stands on its own as a structure of art. The

Spenser-Harvey correspondence is a sample of the Ciceronian tradition of Familiar Letters to Friends. Five letters, two by Spenser (under the name Immerito) and three by Harvey (as G. H.), published as "proper, and wittie familiar Letters" in a 70-page pamphlet in 1580 shortly after they were written and just when the two writers were beginning to make their marks.

The letters are full of amiability and playfulness, with a seasoning of vanity and affectation. Spenser quietly brags about his friendship with Sir Philip Sidney and darkly promises to tell about being with Queen Elizabeth. He speaks of the earthquake (of April 6, 1580) that, in London, overthrew "divers old buildings, and peeces of Churches" and asks how it was with Harvey in Cambridge. Harvey responds with a "short, but sharpe, and learned Judgement of Earthquakes." Each attaches poems (some in Latin, some in English) for the other to read and comment on; when Spenser sends no English verses to Harvey, he says in (mock) superiority, "by my Troth, I have no spare time in the World, to thinke on such Toyes." Spenser writes briefly and Harvey very lengthily on problems of versification in English. Each solemnly tells the other that the letter is for him alone, then promptly adds the names of some friends who may or must see it; as Harvey adds to one letter, "Marry I would have those two to see it, as sone as you may conveniently." The reader is given the impression of being let in on a private world in which much of interest and of importance is going on.

Milton's *Of Education* (1644) creates another kind of impression by its form. It is a letter addressed "To Master *Samuel Hartlib*." The form allows Milton to convert what is mainly a detailed statement of educational procedures and goals into a personal document. "I see those aims, those actions which have won you with me," "Neither can I thinke," "I neither ought, nor can in conscience deferre," "I will not resist," "I shall endeavour," "To tell you therefore what I have benefited," "If you can accept of these few observations . . . I here give you them to dispose of"— all of this focus on "I" and "You" (and much more, just on the first page) and so on through the eight pages of the pamphlet. The result is a human treatment of the subject, as between interested friends. While the tone is not cordial, it is always personal and human. It is in the security of that personal tone that Milton is able to make such a gloriously humane remark as "In those vernal seasons of the yeer, when the air is calm and pleasant, it were an injury and sullennesse against nature not to go out, and see her riches, and partake in her rejoycing with heaven and earth." Similarly, Milton can, within this personal form, freely venture to put into words the essence of his own idealism: "The end then of learning is to repair the ruins of our first parents by regaining to know God aright, and out of that knowledge to love him, to imitate him, to be like him, as we may the neerest by possessing our souls of true vertue, which being united to the heavenly grace of faith makes up the highest perfection."

Samuel Hartlib was not a close friend of Milton's, and Hartlib had asked various other Englishmen to give him their ideas on education for publication. Milton was certainly not obliged to cast his thoughts in the form of a letter, but he gained a good deal by doing so. *Of Education* could not very well follow the pattern of Cicero's Familiar Letters to Friends. But it could follow another pattern, that of Seneca's letters, in which the form is exploited to elevate the human basis of the discourse and of the subject. So it is in *Of Education*.

Lord Chesterfield's substantial achievements as a diplomat and statesman have been eclipsed by the fame of his Letters to his Son. He wrote these letters (some 430 in number) to his only child (an illegitimate son) every couple of weeks when they were apart, from the time the son was about five years old until just before the son died in 1768 at the age of thirty-six. The son's widow published them in 1774, the year after Lord Chesterfield's death.

They were immensely popular, with eleven editions in the first twenty-six years, with many later editions and translations into many foreign languages in the following century or so. The letters continued to be widely read among specialists and non-specialists alike until the early part of this century.

They became a kind of set text that "cultivated" people knew and could refer to in polite society. The Letters to his Son are, in fact, a classic How-To-Do-It manual. The objective is education for worldly success, as a statesman and public figure. Chesterfield tells how he learned the difficult task of living in the world of men and women. With a strong desire to please, he studied to improve his manners, his dress, his conversation, and his general social abilities. He gradually succeeded after strenuous effort and with much help from those who were already perfected in these arts. So can you, he says.

These studies for improvement are the main topics of his Letters to his Son. Nothing is too small for his attention, if it admits of improvement. The son's poor handwriting comes in for repeated and scathingly witty comment, for example. He gives endless testimony on such topics as why certain foreign ministers are more successful than others, the history of the Sorbonne, how long to stay in Hamburg, what Italian authors to read, and the whole truth about individual social and political leaders.

Through the letters runs the theme of the importance of style in achieving the objective of worldly success. Here is how Chesterfield enforced this truth when his son was eighteen:

> I fear, and suspect, that you have taken it into your head, in most cases, that the matter is all, and the manner little or nothing. If you have, undeceive yourself, and be convinced that, in everything, the manner is full as important as the matter. If you speak the sense of an angel, in bad words, and with a disagreeable utterance, nobody will hear you twice, who can help it. If you write epistles as well as Cicero, but in a very bad hand, and very ill-spelled, whoever receives, will laugh at them; and if you had the figure of Adonis, with an awkward air and motions, it will disgust, instead of pleasing. Study manner therefore in everything, if you would be anything. (November 19, 1750)

Even so in the style of prose! The aggressively simplistic manner of these remarks—perhaps suitable for the booby that the son is reputed to have been—is a function of the writer's sense of relation with the reader. All through the letters, the relation (which we are never allowed to forget) is that of the all-knowing Writer/Father/Teacher and the little-knowing Reader/Child/Pupil. The modern reader is involved in this relationship as a close observer and almost as a participant. The mature reader now feels falling on him or her the unsought role of Child and Pupil. It doubtless taxed all the wit and wisdom and worldliness of the writer to make this role endurable in an earlier day, but few readers can now tolerate it. So it is the style, as typified by the relation of the writer and the reader, that has lost these letters their audience.

For one last example of the letter at work by itself as a literary form, John Ruskin. He was certainly a prolific letter writer, and perhaps a great one. Among his published letters are almost two dozen separate volumes to friends and family. It is not surprising that he should also use the form of the letter to set forth, to the world at large, ideas that were of the greatest consequence to him.

For example, *Fors Clavigera* (1871–1884), which is a series of ninety-six letters, issued monthly in pamphlet form and collected in eight volumes; in the Cook and Wedderburn edition, they occupy three fat volumes. Ruskin wrote *Fors Clavigera* to ease his own sense of misery at the social disease that he felt in the world, and the work rotates around social reform. But its music is like the sound of a one-man band, with many different voices speaking out, one after another, on a multitude of topics. His use of the letter form made this multiplicity more comprehensible, and the tones that the letters admit made it more engaging.

Here is the somber opening of the first letter, dated January 1, 1871, the beginning of a new decade: "Friends,—We begin to-day another group of ten years, not in happy circumstances. Although, for the time, exempted from the direct calamities which have fallen on neighbouring states, believe me, we have not escaped them because of our better deservings. . . ." We are all in this pickle together, and Ruskin (unlike a sermonist) promises us no relief. There are many particulars to our misery. Air pollution, for one. The days are dark, made so by furnace chimneys belching smoke. "It is a new thing for me," says Ruskin, "and a very dreadful one. I am fifty years old, and more; and since I was five, have gleaned the best hours of my life in the sun of spring and summer mornings; and I never saw such as these, till now." He imagines that the smoke is made of dead men's souls. "You may laugh, if you like. I don't believe any one of you would like to live in a room with a murdered man in the cupboard, however well preserved chemically;—even with a sunflower growing out at the top of his head" (Letter 8).

At the same time, there is a strong idealism in Ruskin's proposals. "Well, my friends," he concludes Letter 9, "the final result of the education I want you to give your children will be, in a few words, this. They will know what it is to see the sky. They will know what it is to breathe it. And they will know, best of all, what it is to behave under it, as in the presence of a Father who is in heaven. Faithfully yours, J. Ruskin." Not just talk, either. On one Christmas, he told of making a gift to the public of a tithe of his possessions to a National Fund for the general welfare.

Ruskin's manner toward the reader is often crusty. "You usually read so fast," he says, "that you can catch nothing but the echo of your own opinions, which, of course, you are pleased to see in print. I neither wish to please, nor displease you; but to provoke you to think; to lead you to think accurately; and help you to form, perhaps, some different opinions from those you have now" (Letter 6).

Ruskin gives his reader a little of almost everything. Letters he has received from readers, sometimes with his acerbic answers; long quotations from his favorite writers (like Dante, Sir Thomas More, and Addison); short biographies (as of Sir Walter Scott); fables, stories, sketches (the history of Venice) and recipes (Goose Pie); endless comments on artists; and a great deal of autobiography. It is like a magazine in which all the articles and all the departments are the work of the editor.

This miscellany, this hodgepodge that is *Fors Clavigera*, hangs precariously together because of the form in which Ruskin cast it. The form of the letter gave him the latitude to take up a multitude of topics, to express himself in a multitude of ways, and to subsume them all within one sense of style.

Letters are always teetering on the brink of fiction in their representation of reality. The examples I have given are all, I think, forms of personalizing what is called expository prose. Between expository prose and fiction there is a borderland that may be illustrated by Oliver Goldsmith's *Citizen of the World*, his "Chinese Letters" of 1760–61, in which the foreign traveler writes letters home, describing and criticizing the strange customs he meets with in England; the book is satire both in an expository mode and also in a fictive mode.

Although fiction is outside of the scope of our inquiry, these comments on letters would be incomplete without at least an allusion to the major role that letters have been given in fiction. The epistolary novel was at one time thought of by critics as an

18th-century phenomenon because of *Pamela, Clarissa, Humphry Clinker,* and the rest; moreover, it is estimated that the epistolary novel made up about a fifth of all English fiction of the 18th century. But the awareness has been growing for some years now that the letter has been a significant form in all fiction in English from the middle of the 16th century to Saul Bellow and beyond. In fiction, too, the letter has an important role in setting a relation between the writer and the reader and in establishing a style.

III

The letter also frequently serves in an auxiliary role in helping to form the relation of the writer and the reader and thus establish the style. Letters as preliminary addresses to the reader, for example, or open dedications of a text, when the body of the work itself is not in the form of letters. The way we read these letters will affect the way we understand the text that follows.

We may forget how habitual this use of the letter was in English, particularly in the centuries after the introduction of printing, with William Caxton as a notable 15th-century practitioner of the art. In the 16th and 17th centuries, for example, preliminary letters were so usual in printed books (except for ephemeral pamphlets and official publications) that they seem a normal arrangement. The practice continued, of course, though its use has become more limited in recent times. Since our concern at the moment is with tradition and its continuing impact, let me make a few comments on some exemplary texts before 1700.

The most common arrangement of prefatory letters was first a Dedicatory Epistle (one or more) and then a letter To the Reader. If we read these texts in modern editions or anthologies, we may discover that some or all of the prefatory letters are omitted; when they are present, we may think about them as a detachable and optional part of the text. That would be a disaster for a reading of *The Anatomy of Melancholy* or *A Tale of A Tub,* and a distortion for many texts. The Letter to the Reader was normally considered to be a part of the text in the times of which we are speaking. On the title page of *Willobie His Avisa* (1594), for example, the following direction appears: "Read the preface to the Reader before you enter farther." Moreover, when texts were reprinted, the prefatory letters were normally included, even if they were out of date. Prefatory letters are in fact an integral part of the text in the sense that they help to tune the reader to the text by opening up the relation between himself and the writer and by establishing the style.

Often a prefatory letter defines the audience and gives a sense of the personality of the writer and of his purpose. This is the case with Roger Ascham's *Toxophilus* (1545). After a dedicatory epistle to King Henry VIII, Ascham addresses a letter "To all Gentle men and Yomen of Englande," in which he asserts his own personal commitment to

> the shotyng in the long bowe, for English men: which thyng with all my hart I do wish, and if I were of authoritie, I wolde counsel all the gentlemen and yomen of Englande, not to chaunge it with any other thyng, how good soever it seme to be: but that styll, accordyng to the oulde wont of England, youth shulde use it for the moost honest pastyme in peace, that men myght handle it as a mooste sure weapon in warre.

With this kind of involvement, he goes on to explain why he wrote *Toxophilus* and what he hopes its effect will be on any of us who read it:

> For this purpose I, partelye provoked by the counsell of some gentlemen, partly moved by the love whiche I have alwayes borne towarde shotyng, have wrytten this lytle treatise, wherein if I have not satisfyed any man, I trust he wyll the rather be content with my doying, bycause I am (I suppose) the firste, whiche hath sayde any thynge in this matter (and fewe begynninges be perfect, sayth wise men). . . . My minde is, in profityinge and pleasynge every man, to hurte or displease no man, intendying none other purpose, but that youthe myght be styrred to labour, honest pastyme, and vertue.

With such an amiable explanation, as from one human being to another, it would be hard not to respond favorably to the "lytle treatise" set before us. Ascham felt it important to tell us how he happened to write a book, and this telling is important in establishing the relation between us.

John Lyly's manner in addressing the readers of his two Euphues books (1578 and 1580) is very different from that of Ascham, and of a sort that took a number of forms in many other writers. Lyly is conventionally defensive about his books, and he studies to encourage a favorable reaction to them. Readers are implicitly divided into two classes: those favorably disposed (courteous readers, the wise) and those opposed (curious sifters, fools). An adversarial relation is set up with the latter, and readers are encouraged to join him in this conflict with folly. The title page of his second Euphues book epitomizes his relation to readers with this short slogan: "Commend it, or amend it."

Dedicatory epistles also help to set us on the track. The dedicatory letter in front of Sir Philip Sidney's *Arcadia* (1590) opens the family circle of the Sidneys to the reader:

> To My Deare Ladie and Sister, the Countesse of Pembroke
> Here now have you (most deare, and most worthy to be most deare Lady) this idle worke of mine: which I fear (like the Spiders webbe) will be thought fitter to be swept away, then worn to any other purpose. . . . Read it then at your idle tymes, and the follyes your good judgement wil finde in it, blame not, but laugh at. And so, looking for no better stuffe, then, as in a Haberdashers shoppe, glasses, or feathers, you will continue to love the writer, who doth excedinglie love you; and most most hartelie praies you may long live, to be a principall ornament to the familie of the Sidneis.
>
> > Your loving Brother
> > Philip Sidnei.

In this short preamble to the *Arcadia,* we feel that we are being privileged to read a private communication between two persons of consequence. (It is no matter whether Sidney intended this letter to go only with what we style the Old Arcadia; here it is, and it has become part of the text that we call "The Countess of Pembroke's Arcadia.") The air of negligence ("idle worke" fit for "idle tymes") we perceive as the conventional attitude of a Renaissance gentleman-maker. What is most striking is the open and affectionate warmth of Sidney's letter. This expression of love must certainly engage the personal feelings of most readers.

And this style helps to set our inner attitude toward what is to follow.

Since dedicatory epistles were commonly addressed to personages of honor, the association with the dedicatee tends to dignify the text, particularly at a time when class structures are prominent and valued, or for readers (most of us, probably) who are struck by status. In dedicating his translation of Plutarch's *Lives* (1579) to Queen Elizabeth, Sir Thomas North joined a goodly company of dedicators to that queen, a company that ultimately numbered more than two hundred. (Only Charles I seems to have drawn more dedications, at a time when a great many more books were being published.) The whole of the first edition of Bacon's *Advancement of Learning* (1605) was addressed to James I, each of the two books being a kind of long letter as an offering to the king; but the tone of each letter, notably personal to begin with, turns into impersonality after the first few pages. Bishop Joseph Hall perhaps wins the prize for the most dedications jammed into a single book: his *Works* (1625 and later editions) is dedicated as a whole to James I, but it contains some fifty separate treatises, almost every one of them with its own dedicatory epistle to a different person and sometimes also with a Letter to the Reader. Honorable Mention might go to Aemilia Lanyer, whose *Salve Deus* (1611) opens with eleven different dedicatory epistles that take up more than a third of the pages of her book.

To return to prefatory Letters to the Reader, John Florio's translation of Montaigne's *Essays* (1603) begins with Florio's own peevish address "To the Curteous Reader" ("if any thinke he could do better, let him trie; then will he better thinke of what is done"). But it then has the marvellously engaging "The Author to the Reader," by Montaigne himself:

> Reader, loe—here a well-meaning Booke. It doth at the first entrance fore-warne thee, that in contriving the same, I have proposed unto myselfe no other then a familiar and private end: I had had no respect or consideration at all, either to thy service, or to my glory . . . it is my selfe I pourtray. My imperfections shall therein be read to the life, and my naturall forme discerned, so farreforth as publike reverence hath permitted me. For,

if my fortune had beene to have lived among those nations, which yet are said to live under the sweete libertie
of Natures first and uncorrupted lawes, I assure thee, I
would most willingly have pourtrayed my self fully and
naked. Thus gentle Reader my selfe am the ground-worke
of my booke: It is then no reason thou shouldest employ
thy time about so frivolous and vaine a subject. Therefore
farewell. From *Montaigne,* the first of March. 1580.

Try to turn away if you can! Montaigne presents himself to the
reader as a secure, self-confident man with a store of resolution
and independence. Take him or leave him. That is the style that
we are asked to carry through the Essays, the style of the man
who said, "When I am playing with my cat, who knows whether
she have more sport in dallying with me then I have in gaming
with her?" (*Essays,* II, 12). The reader can be the cat.

A more affable attitude is taken by Isaak Walton in *The Compleat Angler* (1653), beginning with "To the Reader of this Discourse: But especially, To the honest Angler." His letter is like a
private talk, formal in style but personal in manner. It is a model
example of how a prefatory letter to the reader reveals the nature
of the writer and of the discourse, as well as the role that is
expected of the reader. The letter develops slowly, but it is worth
reviewing at least a short passage (out of half a dozen pages) to
enjoy the flavor and to feel the stylistic effect:

I think fit to tell thee these following truths; that I did
not undertake to write, or to publish this discourse of *fish*
and *fishing,* to please my self, and that I wish it may not
displease others; for, I have confest there are many defects
in it. And yet, I cannot doubt, but that by it, some readers
may receive so much *profit* or *pleasure,* as if they be not
very busie men, may make it not unworthy the time of
their perusall; and this is all the confidence that I can put
on concerning the merit of this Book.

And I wish the Reader also to take notice, that in writing of it, I have made a recreation, of a recreation; and
that it might prove so to thee in the reading, and not to
read *dull,* and *tediously,* I have in severall places mixt some
innocent Mirth; of which, if thou be a severe, sowr com-
plexioned man, then I here disallow thee to be a com-

petent Judg. . . . And I am the willinger to justifie this *innocent Mirth,* because the whole discourse is a kind of picture of my owne disposition, at least of my disposition in such daies and times as I allow my self, when honest *Nat.* and *R. R.* and I go a fishing together; and let me adde this, that he that likes not the discourse, should like the pictures of the *Trout* and other fish, which I may commend, because they concern not my self.

Walton was keenly aware of the presence of the reader, not only in *The Compleat Angler* but also in the prefaces to his lives of Donne, Wotton, Hooker, Herbert, and Sanderson. He conveys his humility and sincerity, and his feeling of concern for the welfare of the reader.

Aphra Behn had an equal interest in the reader, but that interest took a different form. "An Epistle to the Reader," prefaced to her *The Dutch Lover: A Comedy* (1673) is surely one of the most light-hearted, teasing addresses ever made to readers. Here is how it begins:

Good, Sweete, Honey, Sugar-candied READER.

(Which I think is more than any one has call'd you yet.) I must have a word or two with you before you do advance into the Treatise; but 'tis not to beg your pardon for diverting you from your affairs, by such an idle Pamphlet as this is, for I presume you have not much to do, and therefore are to be obliged to me for keeping you from worse imployment, and if you have a better, you may get you gone about your business: but if you will mispend your time, pray lay the fault upon your self; for I have dealt pretty fairly in the matter, and told you in the Title Page what you are to expect within. Indeed, had I hung out a sign of the Immortality of the Soul, of the Mystery of Godliness, or of Ecclesiastical Policie, and then had treated you with Indiscerpibility, and Essential Spissitude (words, which though I am no competent Judge of, for want of Languages, yet I fancy strongly ought to mean just nothing) with a company of Apocryphal midnight tales cull'd out of the choicest insignificant Authors. . . . But having inscrib'd Comedy on the beginning of my

Book, you may guess pretty near what peny-worths you are like to have, and ware your money and your time accordingly.

And she rattles on and on for eight or nine pages of friendly banter about current comedies and acting, but always with the reader clearly in mind, and setting the style for a way to read her play.

For one final example, of yet another sort, "The Epistle to the Reader" of John Locke's *An Essay Concerning Human Understanding* (1690). Locke begins with a little explanation of the occasion for writing, a hope for the reader's pleasure, and a denial that he is commending himself:

Reader, I here put into thy Hands, what has been the diversion of some of my idle and heavy Hours: If it has the good luck to prove so of any of thine, and thou hast but half so much Pleasure in reading, as I had in writing it, thou wilt as little think thy Money, as I do my Pains ill bestowed. Mistake not this, for a Commendation of my Work; nor conclude, because I was pleased with the doing of it, that therefore I am fondly taken with it now it is done.

Then a little dissertation on the pleasures of thinking for yourself and forming your own judgment. Finally, an avowal that the book will stand or fall on the basis of the opinion of the reader, not that of the writer:

If thou judgest for thy self, I know thou wilt judge candidly; and then I shall not be harmed or offended, whatever be thy Censure. For though it be certain, that there is nothing in this Treatise of whose Truth I am not persuaded; yet I consider my self as liable to Mistakes, as I can thinke thee; and know that this Book must stand or fall with thee, not by any Opinion I have of it, but thy own.

Locke pairs himself personally with the reader. Both are liable to error. Both have opinions of the book—but those of the reader count for most.

What Swift might have said ironically, Locke says sincerely:

"It will possibly be censured as a great piece of Vanity, or Insolence in me, to pretend to instruct this our knowing Age." (We think of that "knowing American" in "A Modest Proposal" who is so well versed in cooking year-old children.) But Locke keeps coming back to his possible failure to please some readers, and he offers several kinds of apology, including one against the charge—perhaps surprising to most modern readers—that there is little new in the book for those who are reasonably well informed:

> If thou findest little in it new or instructive to thee, thou art not to blame me for it. It was not meant for those who had already mastered this Subject, and made a thorough Acquaintance with their own Understandings; but for my own Information, and the Satisfaction of a few Friends, who acknowledged themselves not to have sufficiently considered it.

The prefatory letters that I have been discussing share many features. They are personal in manner: it is "I" and "You" (not "He" or "She" and "They," much less "One") who are concerned with the subject of the book. They almost always reveal something about the writer, and the writer's hope or fear as to what the reader will feel. In short, the writer appears as a human being, the reader appears as a human being, and they are joined together in a human cause of dealing with a text. If we read these letters as part of the text, the humanizing of the process of reading that results will affect the way we understand the text that follows, sometimes only a little, sometimes a lot. The examples I have mentioned could be multiplied a thousand times, or a thousand thousand times. The principle would, I believe, remain the same: in texts of this sort, the relation of the writer and the reader goes far toward establishing the style.

IV

Many other forms of writing, most of them with shorter histories than the letter, go to make up the written tradition of expository prose. Those with a semi-personal cast tend to remove some of the distance between the writer and the reader—the space that intervenes in what we consider "ordinary" expository prose. I am thinking of the dialogue, the autobiography, and the personal essay. Since these forms have continued to be familiar in their basic design, I would like to offer only a quick reminder, through a few examples, of how they work stylistically in humanizing the text and bringing the reader closer to the writer.

The dialogue, the most ancient of them, looks back to the Dialogues of Plato (and ultimately to the non-surviving Sicilian mimes) and to Lucian's *Dialogues of the Dead,* and across the way to the drama and fiction. The form has been used sporadically throughout our literary history; it was much practised in Italy in the late 16th and early 17th centuries, and in France a century later. A cross section of notable English examples might include such works as More's *Utopia* (1516), Walton's *Compleat Angler* (1653), Dryden's *Essay of Dramatick Poesie* (1668), and Landor's *Imaginary Conversations* (1824–1852). In the first three examples I have mentioned, the form is used mainly to express ideas; the speakers are of secondary importance. In the last example, the form is used to recreate the past through the combination of character and idea.

Dialogue is, of course, the essential verbal text of plays, and it can make up any desired amount of the texture of fiction. (Mikhail Bakhtin has argued that dialogue is a basic category of language.) When dialogue is used as a conventional form for expository prose, the expression of ideas or character is normally of paramount importance.

Dialogues achieve their effect by simulating conversation, a characteristic human art. The result, in the hands of an able writer, is a representation of reality in terms that have a natural appeal because it appears to be human rather than ideational, and most all of us (even the more intellectual sort) are more readily drawn to people than we are to ideas.

For example, near the beginning of the *Utopia,* thievery is under discussion at the Cardinal's dinner table. An argument ensues between Raphael and a layman learned in the law, on such matters as why the number of thieves is so large, whether the laws against thievery are just, whether thievery can be reduced by severe punishment, and the like. The two speakers clash in argument, and out of their disagreement More is able to set forth, entirely by the dialogue, a persuasive view about the injustice of the laws against thievery and the need for more fundamental action. It is the more attractive because we are free to make a choice between the positions offered (and implicitly between their proponents); and we are aware that some people (overly rigid and conservative, we might think) will be inclined to choose the views of the layman learned in the law.

The distance between the writer and the reader is naturally shortened when the writer tells about him or her self in the text. This happens most obviously in autobiography. The literature of autobiography is extremely rich. A mere glance at the listings under Autobiography in the *Cambridge Bibliography of English Literature* is somewhere between impressive and overwhelming, even though the later volumes throw Autobiography in with journals, diaries, and letters. We may remind ourselves of the variety of ways in which the form has been used by recalling a few examples.

Margaret Cavendish, Duchess of Newcastle (1623–1673) wrote hers to please herself by giving a free and ingenuous account of her birth, breeding, and life. It is her effort to tell the truth (about her own singularity and fearfulness, for example) that draws us to her and helps to open her book to us.

John Bunyan's *Grace Abounding* (1666) is, on the other hand, a spiritual autobiography, entirely personal and intimate. He encourages the reader to make a similar self-examination for the benefit of his own everlasting welfare.

John Stuart Mill's *Autobiography* (1873) is a history of his mind, of his "unusual and remarkable" education, of the successive phases of his intellectual development. Its openness engenders admiration, but it does not involve us very deeply as human beings.

In Anthony Trollope's *Autobiography* (1883), the intellect plays little part; the writer and his writings have the center stage. He tells about himself with straightforward sincerity, as the diligent man who has to write 10,000 words a week while holding a full-time job and riding to hounds several times a month. "I never fancied myself," he wrote, "to be a man of genius."

Thomas Merton's *The Seven Storey Mountain* (1948) is an open, personal account of his life up to the age of thirty-three, when he takes his solemn vows as a Trappist monk. Ordinary events are connected by the spiritual theme of learning to do God's will, and the book becomes a more and more explicit address to the reader as it approaches its climax.

In Leonard Woolf's five volumes of autobiography (1960–1969), he seems to hold nothing back in giving a truthful picture of himself, the people he knew, and the society in which he lived. It is as if he had made a contract of honesty with the reader, which he fulfills (for example) in his account of Virginia Woolf's death. It all seems personal and genuine.

Personal and genuine are expectations that the reader commonly brings to autobiography. If it is not personal, then there is a distance in feeling between the writer and the reader. If it does not seem genuine, then there is a gap in confidence between the writer and the reader. Sometimes those can be overcome, but only by the reader exceeding his part of the contract, which is to read with as much openness and understanding as he can muster for the occasion.

Sometimes the writer focusses on one feature, like the Duchess of Newcastle on breeding, Mill on the intellect, Trollope on the ordinary. Sometimes the writer goes beyond his part of the contract by trying to persuade the reader to a belief or an action that might not come naturally to him. Bunyan, for example, wants the reader to recall the episodes in his or her own spiritual growth. Merton wants to persuade the reader to share the fruits of contemplation and gain spiritual vitality. With Woolf, you are on your own, to believe or not as you think best. For him, after death nothing is; but what you believe about that matter is your own business and not the concern of Leonard Woolf. However it goes, the relation establishes a style.

The tradition of the informal or personal essay has been very strong in English letters since the Renaissance. A tiny cross section might include Cowley and Temple from the 17th century, Steele and Addison from the 18th, Lamb and Hazlitt from the 19th, and Beerbohm and Thurber from the early 20th century.

Charles Lamb has long been the most celebrated personal essayist in our language. Consider the tactics evident in a handful of his best-known essays in setting the relation and the style.

Often the very first sentence comes right out of the essay and grabs the reader by the arm. "I have an almost feminine partiality for old china," begins "Old China." "When I go to see any great house, I inquire for the china-closet, and next for the picture gallery." Or the opening of "My Relations": "I am arrived at that point of life at which a man may account it a blessing, as it is a singularity, if he have either of his parents surviving." Or, for another family beginning, "Mackery End, in Hertfordshire": "Bridget Elia [his sister Mary] has been my housekeeper for many a long year. I have obligations to Bridget, extending beyond the period of memory. We house together, old bachelor and maid, in a sort of double singleness." In these essays, and in others of a similar cast, Lamb establishes an immediate relation with the reader by blurting out something personal or private or intimate about himself.

Sometimes the relation is established by making a confession of weakness. In "Imperfect Sympathies," for example, he confesses his prejudice against Scotchmen, Jews, and Quakers. "A Chapter on Ears" confesses (after playing with the joke as to whether he is "by nature destitute of those exterior twin appendages") the fact that he has no ear for music. Or his confession of ignorance, in "The Old and the New Schoolmaster," that "My reading has been lamentably desultory and immethodical" and that he is entirely uninformed about science, modern languages, and a multitude of other subjects.

Many of us, as readers, share one or another of the weaknesses he imputes to himself. Sometimes he combines a description of himself with an inference about the reader's condition, as he does in the beginning of "The Superannuated Man": "If peradventure, Reader, it has been thy lot to waste the golden years of thy life—thy shining youth—in the irksome confinement of an office; to have thy prison days prolonged through middle age down to decrepitude and silver hairs, without hope of release or respite; to have lived to forget that there are such things as holidays, or to remember them but as the prerogatives of childhood; then, and then only, will you be able to appreciate my deliverance." Or the beginning of his account of where he once worked, in "The South-Sea House": "Reader, in thy passage from the Bank—where thou hast been receiving thy half-yearly dividends (supposing thou art a lean annuitant like myself)—to the Flower Pot, to secure a place for Dalston, or Shacklewell, or some other thy suburban retreat northerly—didst thou never observe a melancholy-looking, handsome brick and stone edifice, to the left—where Threadneedle Street abuts upon Bishopsgate?"

Because of his various ways of establishing a close relation with the reader, Lamb seems an especially human writer and a particularly appealing person. So much so, that many readers (I believe) are as interested in him as a human being as in his writings, perhaps more so. Which, from the point of view of letters, is very much like another distemper of learning.

The personal element can find a place in many other kinds of writing as well as the essay. In biography, for example. To allude to a few notable biographies that incorporate a personal element of the writer's life. William Roper introduces himself in his *Life of Sir Thomas More, Knight* (1557?/1626) as More's son-in-law, resident in his house for sixteen years, more understanding of More's doings than any other living person; and he proceeds to give a personal account of More. George Cavendish puts himself into his *Life and Death of Thomas Wolsey* (1557?/1641) and gives an "I" view of Wolsey as his "lord and master" until death. Izaak Walton writes his *Life of Dr. John Donne* (1640) as a friend and neighbor, and he allows himself and his piety to give strong color to the biography. James Boswell's *Life of Samuel Johnson* (1791) is in some particulars as much a life of the biographer as of the biographee.

The sense of the writer can, in fact, make itself known to the reader in any kind of writing. Wherever that happens, within the personal written tradition, our understanding of the text is affected.

How it is affected depends on the kind of relation that the writer sets up for the reader, and what quality of response is within the power of the reader. Bunyan, for example, connects himself with the reader by revealing the intimate details of his own personal spiritual struggles with sin. These struggles were of crucial and ultimate importance to him in the quest for salvation.

How is the reader's understanding of the text affected? It depends on the individual reader, of course. Is he or she sympathetic, indifferent, or antagonist to the values that Bunyan builds the relation on? Is the reader on this occasion docile, independent, introspective, froward, amiable, zealous, unconventional, frolicsome, or whatever combination of qualities it might take to define that reader at this moment and to give a basis for speculating as to how he or she will react to the hand that Bunyan holds out to him? There are no easy answers. But the answers are crucial, even about the self. And the answers turn on the degree to which we are capable of perceiving style, the ways that we can read the text, and the understanding that can consequently come to us from our reading.

8.

THE RELATION OF THE WRITER AND THE READER
The Impersonal Tradition

A mathematical formula is the perfection of impersonality. For those who know the signs, the meaning of the formula can be separated from any emotional involvement with the signs. And the meaning itself can be entirely unambiguous.

Since verbal signs are always potentially ambiguous, it takes a special effort to stabilize the way that readers will understand them. This result is obviously desirable in the case of public laws, highway signs, private legal documents, reports of scientific experiments, and the like. Some degree of stabilization is advantageous in most verbal communications of fact and associated opinion, like a weather forecast, a report of a football game, or notes on the distribution of anti-ballistic missiles.

One common method of trying to stabilize the way that readers will understand a text is the resort to impersonality. If the emotions of the writer and the reader are minimized, the emphasis will then fall on the subject of the discourse. Most formal expository prose, such as studies of literature or culture or language or people, has generally tended to exemplify the impersonal tradition of writing.

I would like, first of all, to give a little sketch of the backgrounds of the impersonal tradition of expository prose. Next, to examine, within this tradition, some brief samples of writings by three notable practitioners—Francis Bacon, Samuel Johnson, and Matthew Arnold. Finally, to review some passages from the expository writings of widely influential critics and scholars of the earlier part of this century—T. S. Eliot, I. A. Richards, Northrop Frye, Wayne C. Booth, and Walter J. Ong. Throughout, my concern is to try to identify what kinds of relations between writer and reader may be perceived within the impersonal tradition. And how these relations affect our sense of the style and hence the way we read and perform the texts.

I

From the capacious body of Greek writings, let me single out just two examples that may represent some central strands of the impersonal tradition. First, Heraclitus (fl. 500 B.C.). The series of thoughts that make up the body of his extant writings read somewhat like aphorisms. Here is one from near the beginning: "Bad witnesses are eyes and ears to men, if they have souls that understand not their language" (IV). The Greeks who had the complete body of Heraclitus's writings called him "the dark," presumably from such a saying as this one: "Nature is wont to hide herself" (X).

Heraclitus is concerned with what he regards as the basic and elementary forces of the cosmos, especially fire; but his thought commonly turns toward human behavior. Here is a final example taken from near the end of what we have left of his writings: "It is hard to contend against one's heart's desire; for whatever it wishes to have it buys at the cost of soul" (CV).

Heraclitus avoids the use of narrative and imperative, and he minimizes a discourse of "I" and "You" and "We." His most common form is put into English in the third person of "He" and "They," our impersonal mode. The impersonal tradition is assertive in manner. It allows for few questions except those that direct their own answer. It minimizes the use of subordinated speakers or human byplay. Heraclitus's special style, within the impersonal tradition, is terse, condensed, aphoristic, gnomic.

Heraclitus is an early Greek exemplar of the tradition of wisdom literature, with its roots deep in Egyptian and oriental culture, at least as far back as the third millennium B.C. This tradition, which is probably common to all cultures, has continued to have a dominant place in eastern thought, and it is evident (though mostly in a subordinate role) in western thought as well. With us, relatively few people—like George Herbert, Benjamin Franklin, and William Blake—are content to let aphoristic statements stand alone to carry out their purposes; hence, perhaps, our puzzled response to Chinese expressions of that nature all the way from Confucius to Chairman Mao.

When we English-speaking people think of wisdom literature, what usually come to our minds are the wisdom books of the Old Testament (Proverbs, Job, and Ecclesiastes, in particular). The motto of Proverbs is a familiar example: "The fear of the Lord is the beginning of knowledge: but fools despise wisdom and instruction" (i.7). The seeker in Proverbs has several steps set before him, and the sequence seems to be: instruction—knowledge—understanding—wisdom. Wisdom, the apex, is usually expressed in the form of a saying or an aphoristic thought. But it is meant—in Heraclitus, in Proverbs, in the wisdom literature generally—to open up and express an essence of the culture of the civilization it represents. This idea is, I believe, central to the aphoristic writing within the impersonal tradition.

The other form of impersonal texts to which I would like to refer can be called the treatise. The unsurpassed composer of them among the Greeks was Aristotle (384–322 B.C.), with forty-odd treatises that bear his name. The one of most interest to most literary students has been the *Poetics*. A brief passage can remind us of Aristotle's tactics in defining, analyzing, describing, categorizing, and seeking causes. Here he is on tragedy:

> Tragedy is, then, a representation of an action that is heroic and complete and of a certain magnitude—by means of language enriched with all kinds of ornament, each used separately in the different parts of the play: it represents men in action and does not use narrative, and through pity and fear it effects relief to these and similar emotions. (Section vi, Loeb Library, Fyfe translation)

Although Aristotle is not always so entirely impersonal as he is in this passage, his deviations are not in fact very personal. What counts for most—what attention is focussed on—is the subject, not the writer or the reader.

The writing of treatises was such a common practice among the down-to-earth Romans that it is hard to single out one example for comment. But Pliny the Elder (A.D. 23–79) certainly deserves recognition for the length and scope of his treatise on *Natural History* (ten Loeb volumes, and encyclopedic in nature). Here is his brief account of petroleum, which was a useless curiosity in the ancient world:

> In Samosata the capital of Commagene there is a marsh that produces an inflammable mud called petroleum. When this touches anything solid it sticks to it; also when people touch it, it actually follows them as they try to get away from it. By these means they defended the city walls when attacked by Lucullus: the troops kept getting burnt by their own weapons. Water merely makes it burn more fiercely; experiments have shown that it can only be put out by earth. (Book II, section cviii)

Pliny made notes from thousands of books as the basis for his treatise. He was particularly attracted by the marvellous and the unusual in the realm of people, animals, plants, and the physical world. He records about a thousand facts, investigations, and authorities in each of his thirty-seven books. He covers the widest possible range of details, from the instinctive sense of danger in wild animals, to remedies for indigestion, to the views of magicians about moles on the human body, to methods of killing ants in gardens, to affection among snakes, to signs of impending earthquakes.

The interest and amusement in Pliny derive almost entirely from the topics that he treats and the information that he purveys. Not from any sense of personal involvement on the part of the reader, nor from any effort on Pliny's part to present himself or to establish any relation with the reader.

Yet, somehow, at least a glimmering of the writer contrives to come through, even in the impersonal tradition, if we read enough of the writings of an author with attention. The impersonal tradition itself imparts an element of authority to the writer because he or she is telling us what is or what was or what may be or what is not. This is a role that some writers seem to relish, and they fill it more fully than necessity requires.

A word about the way in which the writers I have just quoted appear to me as a reader, judging as far as possible only from their impersonal writings. Heraclitus seems self-confident, single-minded, contemptuous, and arrogant. Aristotle seems clear-headed, shrewd, systematic, and categorical. Pliny seems open-minded, credulous, inquisitive, and erudite. Those are my impressions. What are yours? They may be different, but they doubtless exist and can be verbalized. And they have a bearing on how we read the texts of these writers.

II

The opening of Donne's poems are often strikingly memorable.
Here are the familiar lines with which a few of his Holy Sonnets
begin:

Batter my heart, three-person'd God; for, you . . .

I am a little world made cunningly . . .

Death be not proud, though some have called thee . . .

At the round earth's imagin'd corners, blow . . .

Spit in my face you Jews, and pierce my side . . .

Thou hast made me, and shall thy work decay? . . .

Show me, dear Christ, thy Spouse, so bright and clear . . .

Oh my black Soul! now thou art summoned . . .

The opening of Bacon's writings are often strikingly memorable. Here are the familiar lines with which a few of his Essays
begin:

Men fear Death, as children fear to go in the dark . . .
("Of Death")

Revenge is a kind of wild justice . . . ("Of Revenge")

The joys of parents are secret; and so are their griefs and
fears . . . ("Of Parents and Children")

He that hath wife and children hath given hostages to
fortune . . . ("Of Marriage and Single Life")

It were better to have no opinion of God at all, than such
an opinion as is unworthy of him . . . ("Of Supersti-
tion")

Suspicions amongst thoughts are like bats amongst birds,
they ever fly by twilight . . . ("Of Suspicion")

Virtue is like a rich stone, best plain set . . . ("Of Beauty")

God Almighty first planted a Garden . . . ("Of Gardens")

Studies serve for delight, for ornament, and for ability . . .
("Of Studies")

These openings by Donne and Bacon are striking, and they
are memorable. They invite us to go on and read the remainder

of the sonnet or the essay. They vividly illustrate two traditions: Donne and the personal tradition, Bacon and the impersonal tradition.

The openings that I have quoted from Donne are all personal. They are generally in the first or second persons: the speaker of the poem is talking in his own person about himself, or he is making a petition in the imperative, or he is addressing another or a part of himself. These openings—and the poems that follow—are all decisively personal. In speaking personally, they also speak to us as fellow human beings.

The openings that I have quoted from Bacon are all impersonal. They are all in the third person, and there is no specified speaker. They are all assertions of opinion directed at the world at large. They are spoken on behalf of enunciating a truth. Their appeal is intellectual, and they speak to us as human beings who have a concern for knowing more or better truths than we have known before.

Bacon continues the impersonal manner right through his Essays, with only infrequent personal expressions (such as "I am sure," "we see," "I think"), but they do not disrupt the impersonal effect. (Only "Of Building" and "Of Gardens" make considerable use of the first person, and these two pieces seem more like directions for constructing a house and a garden for his personal use than like essays.)

Bacon's manner is condensed and balanced. It runs toward aphoristic statement, and the brief and concise assertions are sometimes received into the fold of the world's book of aphorisms. The *Oxford Book of Aphorisms* (1983), for example, contains twenty aphorisms from Bacon's Essays scattered through the book. Bacon's mind and his expression seem always to run toward the aphorism. It was a form that he developed for his scientific work. What we have of the *Magna Instauratio* and its *Novum Organum* consist mainly of what Bacon called "aphorisms"— really succinct paragraphs that digest into summary form the argument of what might otherwise have been a treatise.

To return to the Essays. Bacon's aphoristic style has been popular among those who quote memorable statements. The *Oxford Book of Quotations* (3d edn., 1979) devotes five columns (twenty-two separate entries) to quotations from Bacon's Essays, for the most part not the aphorisms that appear in the other book; the largest number of these quotations—seven—are from "Of Studies." The old familiar Bartlett's *Familiar Quotations* (14th edn., 1968) prints thirty-nine quotations from Bacon's Essays, but "Of Adversity" wins the prize this time, with five entries, over three from "Of Studies."

"Of Studies" is, in fact, a model example of the impersonal tradition in its purest form. Most of the sentences that make up this short essay of less than five hundred words—one or two pages in most books—remain comfortable in the memory and continue their work. Sentences like these:

Studies serve for delight, for ornament, and for ability.

To spend too much time in studies is sloth; to use them too much for ornament is affectation; to make judgement wholly by their rules is the humour of a scholar.

Crafty men contemn studies, simple men admire them, and wise men use them.

Read not to contradict and confute; nor to believe and take for granted; nor to find talk and discourse; but to weigh and consider.

Some books are to be tasted, others to be swallowed, and some few to be chewed and digested.

Reading maketh a full man; conference a ready man; and writing an exact man.

Histories make men wise, poets witty, the mathematics subtile, natural philosophy deep, moral grave, logic and rhetoric able to contend.

Nay there is no stond or impediment in the wit, but may be wrought out by fit studies.

These few sentences—which actually make up nearly a third of the entire essay—offer their thoughts with quiet certainty, but without argumentation. Any reader who was roused into contentiousness could debate the truth of any of these sentences endlessly. I believe that readers of this essay do not, generally, feel inclined to dispute its issues, and this is testimony to the sense of fairness that is perceived in Bacon's way of handling the impersonal tradition. And of his wish for his ideas to "come home to men's business and bosoms."

142

This whole essay—and indeed a great deal of Bacon's writings in general—is in the tradition of wisdom literature. The writer is the "wise man" (venerated in many cultures, though not much in ours), revealing the secrets of his deepest thoughts. What the wise man says, and what Bacon says, has a little of the cast of the oracular or prophetic about it.

Bacon's essay "Of Friendship" is a good example of a different use of the impersonal tradition. Readers of Cicero and Montaigne might naturally turn to a comparison of their essays on friendship with Bacon's, and the comparison is revealing.

Cicero's "De Amicitia" (44 B.C.) is in the form of a dialogue between Lelius and his two young sons-in-law. Cicero was a student of the law under one of the sons-in-law when the latter was a very old man. Cicero says that he is repeating the dialogue as it was told him by that old man.

It is a warm, human story that centers on the friendship between Lelius and Scipio Africanus. Scipio has recently died, and Lelius tells about their friendship and the ties that make possible all friendship, which is derived from love. Love, in turn, is based on awareness of and admiration for virtue. Since virtue lies at the heart of all true friendship, only honorable acts can be justly done in support of friends. Virtue knits friendship together, and the deepest kind of friendship can exist only among really good men. Virtue, in short, is the basis for friendship and all other desirable things, including the best and highest goal, which (in Cicero's view) is happiness.

The dialogue moves along through the give and take of conversation. People are telling other people about themselves and their friends and their ideas about love and virtue and friendship. The manner of the dialogue is entirely human and personal.

Montaigne's "Of Friendship" (1580), in the form of an essay, is a glowing testimonial to the depth and permanence of the ideal friendship that Montaigne shared with Etienne de La Boétie. Montaigne tells his feelings in the first person, in warmly human direct address to the reader, who may even feel that he is standing in the place of the dead friend. This ideal friendship is based on love, with the souls so mingled and blended that the individual souls cannot be distinguished one from the other. Why such a friendship comes to pass is beyond human understanding, with some inexplicable and fateful force mediating the union. Such a friendship as theirs may occur only once in three centuries.

There are other forms of relationship that go under the name of friendship. They are not true friendship unless they involve a harmony of the wills, which is the boundary of friendship. Montaigne feels that the others are generally nothing but acquaintances formed by some chance or convenience.

Bacon's "Of Friendship" is a quite straightforward and impersonal essay. The major part of it is devoted to setting forth and describing the three principal fruits of friendship: that it brings peace to the affections by helping to ease and discharge tempestuous passions through describing them to a friend, that it gives support to the judgment by resolving confused thoughts through discourse with a friend, and that it provides a person who will give whatever aid you may need in any of your actions and on any occasion. The fruits of friendship are thus practical in the sense that you will gain several things from the friendship and be the better for it. Bacon gives several examples of Roman pairs (like Caesar and Brutus) to show how highly great rulers of the past valued friendship, regardless of the consequences.

The impact of Bacon's essay depends on the logical power of the arguments that are offered. It is as if the essay were written to answer the question as to whether the reader should form a close friendship or not: and the answer is a resounding *Yes*. Bacon takes the practical view, and the impersonal tradition is very suitable for such a presentation.

What can be said about the relation of the writer and the reader in Bacon's essays? Only what is implied, as there are no explicit hints about the writer and the expected reader. The impression that is conveyed by implication, however, is quite strong, even without knowing anything about Bacon. The writer is (it appears) a senior man of affairs, with wide practical experience with people of high place, with much reading, thoughtful, and wise in the ways of the world. His essays are a distillation of his experience with books and with people. He offers these essays to young men who would like to rise in the world. They are not addressed to apprentices or servants or shopkeepers or minor professionals or anybody he would have thought of as a working person. But rather to the bright, energetic person whose situation and drive enabled him to be ambitious to attain a place of consequence in a structured society. That is their style. How we read them depends, in some measure, on how sympathetic we feel to this purpose.

* * * *

Samuel Johnson's prose is one of the great glories of the impersonal tradition. Most of the 320 issues of his composition in *The Rambler, The Adventurer,* and *The Idler* are in that tradition. So are the *Lives of the Poets,* all fifty-two of them. And so also (for smaller but memorable examples) are the "Preface" to *A Dictionary of the English Language* and the "Preface" to *The Plays of William Shakespeare.* I would like for us to try, in the course of a few pages, to explore something of the range of his characteristic forms of discourse in expository prose and of the consequent relation of the writer and the reader of that prose. I do not undertake to offer any other kind of view of Johnson's special achievements or of his possible shortcomings.

His prose has something in common with Bacon's in that they both incline toward the aphorism and toward a search for "abstracted truth." Johnson's prose also inclines toward the moral statement as a natural form of perception, toward balance and antithesis as a natural form of organization, and toward the negative as a natural form of expression.

Johnson was probably just as good an aphorism-maker as Bacon. Johnson's are even more popular, if we can believe the common dictionaries to which I earlier referred. The *Oxford Book of Aphorisms* (1983) has some eighty-four from Johnson, forty-nine of them just from the texts I mentioned above. (For Bacon, there are twenty-eight, of which twenty are from the Essays.) In fact, far more aphorisms are quoted in the *Oxford Book of Aphorisms* from Johnson than from any other writer. Aside from aphorisms, quotations from Johnson are particularly popular, too: the *Oxford Book of Quotations* devotes twenty-one columns to Johnson, and Bartlett about fifteen columns.

What we call aphorisms can be discovered, like small treasures, all through Johnson's prose. "Criticism is a study by which men grow important and formidable at very small expence." So begins *Idler* No. 60. In the course of the "Life of Pope," we find: "He that is pleased with himself, easily imagines that he shall please others." In the middle of *Rambler* No. 32, "The cure for

the greatest part of human miseries is not radical, but palliative."
And in the Preface to Shakespeare, "Nothing can please many,
and please long, but just representations of general nature." Such
sententious assertions as these are the bolts that keep Johnson's
discourse attached to what he thought of as general truth.

In Johnson, as in Bacon, the aphoristic impulse is also at work
in the more diffused discourse that makes up the body of his
prose. Here is a short passage from *Rambler* No. 155: "No weakness of the human mind has more frequently incurred animadversion, than the negligence with which men overlook their own
faults, however flagrant, and the easiness with which they pardon
them, however frequently repeated." It is a deliberate statement
that slowly takes shape before us. Because Johnson is good at
making aphorisms, we may feel that he ought to write in aphorisms whenever possible. An impetuous or impatient person
might wish to go ahead and reduce these thoughts to an aphorism: "No faults are easier to forgive than our own." There. This
translation tightens up the authority of the writer and reduces,
if only a little, the participation of the reader. In the longer
version, various inferences confront the reader, and the inferences tease the reader to come outside and play. On the other
hand, the process of reduction tends to hide the byways of inference and to create a straight road ahead.

Johnson's prose is in the tradition of wisdom literature, but
only loosely so. There are many pure examples like the embed-
ded aphorisms of which I have spoken, and there are even more
of the diffused aphorisms throughout his writings. That feature
may in fact seem more prominent than it actually is, because
aphoristic writing tends to be memorable. Much of the time his
prose has the flavor of wisdom literature without its substance.

In fact, the larger part of his prose is of a different cast. Let
me give, as a single example, this passage from near the end of
the Preface to Shakespeare. Johnson is talking about the work
of the textual critic, here about making conjectural emendations:

> That a conjectural critick should often be mistaken, can-
> not be wonderful, either to others or himself, if it be con-
> sidered, that in his art there is no system, no principal
> and axiomatical truth that regulates subordinate posi-
> tions. His chance of errour is renewed at every attempt;

an oblique view of the passage, a slight misapprehension of a phrase, a casual inattention to the parts connected, is sufficient to make him not only fail, but fail ridiculously; and when he succeeds best, he produces perhaps but one reading of many probable, and he that suggests another will always be able to dispute his claims.

This is what we might call straightforward assertion, of simply telling it the way it is, at least in the view of the writer. In this form, without the explicit personality of a writer or of a reader to humanize the assertions, it characterizes a central stream of the impersonal tradition. The qualifications contained in the passage limit only the province or conditions of the assertion, not the degree of its truth. The nature of the writer is entirely inexplicit. The writer seems to entertain no uncertainty about his assertions, and it seems to be assumed that neither will the reader, once the thoughts have been verbalized and understood.

One other form of discourse that is found in the impersonal tradition (and frequently found in Johnson's prose) is the negative assertion. A simple example is this sentence in the "Life of Dryden": "None of his prefaces were ever thought tedious." This is a lot to swallow all at once, which is a general risk of the unqualified negative. While we are at it, we may be tempted to assume that we are being told that the prefaces were sometimes thought especially interesting (or something of that sort). Although logically we are not being told anything except that none were ever thought tedious, we often feel allowed to take a little more than is being offered, having already been asked to take so much.

In Johnson the negative sometimes is used along with balance or parallelism, as in his assertion about "Lycidas" in the "Life of Milton": "In this poem there is no nature, for there is no truth; there is no art, for there is nothing new." No nature / no truth, no art / nothing new—but no clue as to what is: we are inclined to think we are being told that there's not much of anything else, either.

Here are a couple of famous passages in the negative manner from Johnson's letters. From the celebrated letter to Lord Chesterfield, this triple negative sentence: "I hope it is no very cynical asperity not to confess obligations where no benefit has been received" (February 7, 1755). And this twice-negatived one to Boswell: "You are not to think yourself forgotten, or criminally neglected, that you have had yet no letter from me" (December 8, 1763). But what *was* Boswell to think? That he was remembered? Not exactly, but the negatives give him a push in that direction.

In Johnson's impersonal discourse, what sort of person is implied? It is a difficult question to answer because Johnson is so familiar to us from so many other sources. So far as I can succeed in limiting the source of my answer to his impersonal texts, I would say that the writer is thoughtful, bold, and highly moral. That he is confident and dogmatic but also a little cautious in protecting himself. That he assumes a wide audience of intelligent male and female adults of the middle and upper classes. And that he fully expects his readers to assent to his views and opinions. To the degree that he does not now have such an audience, his impersonal discourse may not succeed in filling those expectations.

* * * *

Matthew Arnold was the master of many forms of discourse. Sometimes he was informal, occasionally flippant, or personal, or ironical, or merry and facetious, or a combination of these and other manners in seeking a hearing or attacking an opponent. His mind seems to have been animated by controversy, but he went for the kill with studied courtesy.

It was mostly in a grave manner that Arnold carried on his role as an Apostle of Culture and a Victorian Sage. This manner tends to work well in the impersonal tradition. It is in this latter manner alone that I wish to have him stand as an exemplar. It is this manner of his, mainly, that made him, for the half century after his death, such an influential critic of literature and society. Let me offer several examples, from the essential body of his prose, as a basis for thinking about how the impersonal tradition works with writers like Arnold.

Here is a paragraph from the middle of the widely-admired Preface to the 1853 edition of Arnold's poems:

The confusion of the present times is great, the multitude of voices counselling different things bewildering, the number of existing works capable of attracting a young writer's attention and of becoming his models, immense. What he wants is a hand to guide him through the confusion, a voice to prescribe to him the aim which he should keep in view, and to explain to him that the value of the literary works which offer themselves to his attention is relative to their power of helping him forward on his road towards this aim. Such a guide the English writer at the present day will nowhere find. Failing this, all that can be looked for, all indeed that can be desired, is, that his attention should be fixed on excellent models; that he may reproduce, at any rate, something of their excellence, by penetrating himself with their works and by catching their spirit, if he cannot be taught to produce what is excellent independently. (*Complete Prose Works*, I [1960], 8–9)

With this form of prose, we are a long way from the aphoristic style so central to Bacon and so frequent in Johnson. To check once more in popular dictionaries, there is only one entry for Arnold in the *Oxford Book of Aphorisms*. His prose is thought memorable in other ways, however, as the *Oxford Dictionary of Quotations* devotes about three columns (some forty entries) to Arnold's prose, and Bartlett five columns (forty-one entries) to it.

This passage is a set of strong assertions as to how the young writer can achieve excellence (Arnold was thirty when he wrote this Preface, and his poems had been made public only within the preceding three or four years.) The passage is clearly explanatory and clearly prescriptive. There is a need: Arnold knows what that need is. There is a solution: Arnold knows what that solution is. All the reader has to do is follow what he is told.

For one other example from Arnold, let me offer a short passage from a late essay, "Wordsworth," first published in 1879 and collected in the posthumous *Essays in Criticism, Second Series* (1888):

It is important, therefore, to hold fast to this: that poetry is at bottom a criticism of life; that the greatness of a poet lies in his powerful and beautiful application of ideas to life,—to the question: How to live. Morals are often treated in a narrow and false fashion; they are bound up with systems of thought and belief which have had their day; they are fallen into the hands of pedants and professional dealers; they grow tiresome to some of us. (*Complete Prose Works*, IX [1973], 46)

Arnold makes the impersonal tradition serve him well in promulgating this statement of idealism. Here he sets up as a judge of poetry and of moral behavior. Within the impersonal tradition, Arnold relies on memorable words and phrases that he allows to stand in summation of some of his central ideas. In this passage, that poetry is a criticism of life; in the passage from the 1853 Preface, the procedure that he was later to call touchstones; and elsewhere, sweetness and light, the best that is known and thought in the world, and others. These catchy words and phrases (slogans almost, or passwords for admission to the circle of the cultivated) focus the reader's attention on key elements of Arnold's thought in his use of the impersonal tradition.

And what does the writer seem like in these passages? To me, he seems like a Teacher, intent on having us learn attitudes and concepts from him. Like a Judge, who is quietly capable of deciding and telling us (as he says in "The Study of Poetry") what is excellent and what is inferior, what is sound, unsound, or half-sound, and what is true, untrue, or half-true. Like a Preacher, who wishes to inspire us to do a lot for ourselves and for society. And the reader? He or she seems to me to be figured as a member of "the great public" that Arnold sought to reach, conventional in training and outlook perhaps, but one who is eager to be a convert to cultivation and to the improvement of him or herself.

The relation of the writer and the reader is, by consequence, a little bit uneasy. All is well so long as the reader fits the figure. But if the reader is (for example) of a more independent spirit, the relationship may either hold together only on historical grounds, or break down under the weight of the perception of the writer as a dogmatist, or suffer some other disability. These are, I think, no more than the normal risks when one tries to impose his or her will on another.

III

Scholars and critics have, in general, adopted the impersonal tradition of discourse. We tell one another what we know or think

or think we know in varying degrees of impersonality. Within
this tradition, however, there is a wide range of possible styles.
Let me offer brief samples from the writings of five notable
critics and scholars of the earlier years of this century. These
samples are from books or essays that have influenced most students of literature in the course of the last couple of generations,
books or essays that may still be influential today, at least at
second hand. As a group, they exemplify (I think) pretty much
the full range of the use of the impersonal tradition in critical
and scholarly writings of their times.

My comments on these passages are intended to be like first
impressions that we may feel if we are reading along with mod-
erate attention and are interrupted: someone asks us to say, on
the basis of this passage alone, a few words about our sense of
the style—our feelings about the author of the text, the reader
who seems to be implied, and the relation between the two. Of
course I don't mean these comments to refer to the writings of
these authors generally, but only to selected passages; with other
passages, the impressions might be different.

Here is the opening of T. S. Eliot's celebrated essay, first published in 1919, called "Tradition and the Individual Talent":

> In English writing we seldom speak of tradition, though
> we occasionally apply its name in deploring its absence.
> We cannot refer to "the tradition" or to "a tradition"; at
> most, we employ the adjective in saying the poetry of So-
> and-so is "traditional" or even "too traditional." Seldom,
> perhaps, does the word appear except in a phrase of cen-
> sure. If otherwise, it is vaguely approbative, with the im-
> plication, as to the work approved, of some pleasing
> archaeological reconstruction. You can hardly make the
> word agreeable to English ears without this comfortable
> reference to the reassuring science of archaeology.

If we assume for the sake of the example that we have had no
prior knowledge of this writer, what can we say about him from
reading this passage alone? We don't know very much about him
on this brief acquaintance, of course, but he seems quick-minded
and self-confident, perhaps a little sharp in making his judg-
ments, with the faint smile from an academic joke on his face in
the last sentence. Under the surface, there may be something of

the Arnoldian tradition of culture operative. How does he figure us as his readers? We are treated a little like interested colleagues in a common inquiry. The discourse is on the "we" level of like-minded associates, not the "we" of royalty. It is the impersonal tradition pressed in the direction of personalness.

Suppose we try to convert this opening to a different style by eliminating the "we" and the "you" in order to see whether our sense of the relation of writer and reader will seem to change. The easiest way is to put it into the passive, like this:

> In English writing, tradition is seldom spoken of, though its name is occasionally applied in deploring its absence. "The tradition" or "a tradition" cannot be referred to; at most, the adjective can be employed in saying that the poetry of So-and-so is "traditional" or even "too traditional." Seldom, perhaps, does the word appear except in a phrase of censure. If otherwise, it is vaguely approbative, with the implication, as to the work approved, of some pleasing archaeological reconstruction. The word can hardly be made agreeable to English ears without this comfortable reference to the reassuring science of archaeology.

The writer has now faded a little further away into the remoteness of impersonality. The reader is given less attention, and the reader is not much involved in the cool conclusions that are being asserted. We have created this difference in style by the conversion of five verbs away from the active form of the first and second persons to the passive voice.

Try the same passage in another way, this time by converting all the first and second persons to the third person:

> In English writing, one seldom speaks of tradition, though one occasionally applies its name in deploring its absence. One cannot refer to "the tradition" or to "a tradition"; at most, one employs the adjective in saying that the poetry of So-and-so is "traditional" or even "too traditional." Seldom, perhaps, does the word appear except in a phrase of censure. If otherwise, it is vaguely approbative, with the implication, as to the work approved, of some pleasing archaeological reconstruction. One can

hardly make the word agreeable to English ears without this comfortable reference to the reassuring science of archaeology.

The effect of this conversion is a slightly different kind of retreat into impersonality. To British ears, it may be a little less impersonal than the passive. To American ears that are not accustomed to hearing what "one" is up to, the feeling of the passage is perhaps just as impersonal as the passive, and also a little mannered. In either case, the substitution of five "one"s for four "we"s and one "you" has created this more impersonal effect.

Here is another example, this time from I. A. Richards's seminal book, *Practical Criticism* (1929). This is the opening paragraph of the body of the book:

> I have set three aims before me in constructing this book. First, to introduce a new kind of documentation to those who are interested in the contemporary state of culture whether as critics, as philosophers, as teachers, as psychologists, or merely as curious persons. Secondly, to provide a new technique for those who wish to discover for themselves what they think and feel about poetry (and cognate matters) and why they should like or dislike it. Thirdly, to prepare the way for educational methods more efficient than those we use now in developing discrimination and the power to understand what we hear and read.

Here the writer presents himself as an authority figure and seems to perceive the reader in a subordinated role, like those hapless undergraduates whose responses are the substance of his book. We can notice that the discourse is in the first and third persons, and a great gulf is fixed between the writer and the reader. "I" and "me" appear in the first sentence, and then all is instrumental to the betterment of "those who." The "we" of the last sentence seems to refer to the writer and his peers, those whom nature has set above us ordinary mortals. The reader is made to feel diminished; he may assume that he or she really belongs in that undifferentiated category of people who are being addressed "merely as curious persons," and is likely to have his knuckles rapped if he wriggles in his seat. The impersonality

153

may be accentuated if we notice that the author set these three aims before himself not in writing but in "constructing this book."

Northrop Frye's *Anatomy of Criticism* was a decisively important book for me (a devoted reader of *Fearful Symmetry*) when it first appeared in 1957. I believe that it meant a great deal to a multitude of readers for at least a decade or two after its publication. Here is the beginning of the last chapter, called "Tentative Conclusion":

> The present book has dealt with a variety of critical techniques and approaches, most of them already used in contemporary scholarship. We have tried to show where the archetypal or mythical critic, the aesthetic form critic, the historical critic, the medieval four-level critic, the text-and-texture critic, belong in a comprehensive view of criticism. Whether the comprehensive view is right or not, I hope some sense has been communicated of what folly it would be to try to exclude any of these groups from criticism. As was said at the beginning, the present book is not designed to suggest a new program for critics, but a new perspective on their existing programs, which in themselves are valid enough.

The passage has an air of almost studied impersonality about it, achieved by the writer generally withdrawing in favor of his book, as if the book had been realized ("reified," we would now say) without human agency or intervention. There is one "we" (of the royal variety) in the second sentence, and an "I hope" moderates an already modest claim in the sentence that follows. On the whole, however, the discourse is strongly passive. The use of "I" is avoided, once at the cost of resorting to the awkward expression "As was said at the beginning." The writer is hard to find, and the reader is even more elusive.

Wayne C. Booth's *Rhetoric of Fiction* has been widely influential since its publication in 1961. This is the way the first chapter begins:

> One of the most obviously artificial devices of the storyteller is the trick of going beneath the surface of the action to obtain a reliable view of a character's mind and heart.

Whatever our ideas may be about the natural way to tell a story, artifice is unmistakably present whenever the author tells us what no one in so-called real life could possibly know. In life we never know anyone but ourselves by thoroughly reliable internal signs, and most of us achieve an all too partial view even of ourselves. It is in a way strange, then, that in literature from the very beginning we have been told motives directly and authoritatively without being forced to rely on those shaky inferences about other men which we cannot avoid in our own lives.

Only the first sentence is in the third person. The other three sentences of this opening paragraph use the first person plural. The passage expresses what is represented as the shared experience of everybody, writer and reader alike. The discourse is not personal, but it is human. The writer creates the impression that he has some thoughts that he wants to share, and that we too will want to share them with him. The topic is represented as interesting for itself, not (as sometimes with Johnson, Arnold, and others) for its instrumental value. With an engaging guide, we probably feel better about ourselves as readers, about the writer, and about the topic.

One final example, of yet another kind of relation of the writer and the reader. Here is the opening paragraph of Walter J. Ong's essay on the relation of writer and audience, called "The Writer's Audience Is Always a Fiction," from his book *Interfaces of the Word: Studies in the Evolution of Consciousness and Culture* (1977):

Although there is a large and growing literature on the differences between oral and written verbalization, many aspects of the differences have not been looked into at all, and many others, although well known, have not been examined in their full implications. Among these latter is the so-called "audience" to writing as such, to the situation that inscribed communication establishes and to the roles that readers as readers are consequently called on to play. Some studies in literary history and criticism at times touch near this subject, but none, it appears, take it up in any historical detail.

Later on in this chapter, we read (p. 74) that "the writer's audience is always a fiction. The historian, the scholar or scientist, and the simple letter writer all fictionalize their audiences, casting them in a made-up role and calling on them to play the role assigned." We may wonder what role has been assigned to us in the passage I quoted. Not, I fear, a role that will flatter our knowledge or our intelligence, but it is hard to be sure. We notice that the discourse is all in the third person (with no "I"s or "You"s or "We"s anywhere in sight), that the dominant voice is passive ("have not been looked into," "have not been examined," "are called on"), and that the presentation is resolutely impersonal ("there is a . . . literature," "Some studies . . . touch near this subject"). It is as if there were no people involved in the grand march of the intellect, but an army of concepts and abstractions were out there tramping up the hill of truth. There is little sense of the writer or the reader here, and the passage is a triumph of impersonality. Still, impersonality is itself both a style and a form of relationship, a cloak that many people find comfortable to wear.

IV

The impersonal tradition covers a lot of ground, and there is no sharp line of demarcation between the personal and the impersonal. Communicating goes on with equal success in both of these traditions, though each has its own congeries of special aptitudes and special uses.

The personal tradition obviously works better when it is important to involve the reader personally and emotionally in the text, in the expectation of deepening his or her understanding of its human implications. The impersonal tradition obviously works better when it is important to avoid, so far as possible, the complications and possible ambiguities and cross currents that are likely to occur when the emotions of the reader are aroused through personal involvement in the text.

In the personal tradition, the writer and the reader are generally identifiable or easily implied. Their relation is usually fairly clear. What comes of that relationship may be very little or very much, conventional or exquisitely complex.

In the impersonal tradition, the writer and the reader are usually not explicitly identifiable. Sometimes they can't be identified at all, as in the rigorous impersonality of legal documents, reports of scientific experiments, and the like. But mostly we can uncover some assumptions, underlying the discourse, about what the writer is like and what the reader is expected to be like. When we aren't told directly what the relation is, we can sense the assumptions and sense the relationship that is implied.

It is true that the impersonal tradition runs, in practice, toward abstraction. It is a refuge for the shy, a platform for the self-assured, a public address system for all whose heart is in the text and who think that impersonality is the best way to get others to understand the text without fear or favor.

There is a wide range of feelings from comfort to discomfort in the impact of the impersonal tradition on the reader, depending on education, experience, and other cultural variables. University-educated Britishers are more comfortable with it than Americans of similar education and background. White Americans are more comfortable with it than black Americans of similar education and background. Older people are more comfortable with it than adolescents, who prefer the second person and the non-demanding imperative. So there are limits and refinements in the way that this—or any other tradition—works.

If we as readers perform a text with feeling and spirit and understanding, we create a dramatic situation and impart a special kind of life to the text. This is true within the personal tradition, of course; but it is also true to some degree, through inference and implication, within the impersonal tradition for all except dehumanized texts. How much of a dramatic situation depends on what the writer has given us to work with and our talent for performance. The dramatic situation itself depends on our implicit understanding of what the writer is like and what role we as readers are playing.

The point is: we are generally feeling *something*, if we are reading with attention. And the something that we feel affects how we respond to the text. Of course it is usually not the controlling feature, and its importance will vary a lot. But it is sometimes, or often, disproportionately important as an emotional reaction: for example, something like appreciation for friendly treatment, something like distaste at being ignored. If we verbalize this feeling, it will usually turn out to be what we articulate as our sense of the style of the text. The result is some kind of modification in our understanding of the text and in our performance of it.

9.

INTERPRETING STYLE
What Else the Text Is Telling Us

How can we learn what else the text is telling us through its style? One way may be to compare what we get from two texts that are trying to convey the same message at widely separated periods of time.

Two texts that answer this description are two translations of the Bible into English. One, the Authorized Version (or the King James Version) published in 1611. The other, the New English Bible, with the New Testament first published in 1961 and the Old Testament in 1970.

These two versions have very much in common. Both were undertaken under high auspices. The Authorized Version (as I shall call it) was made under a mandate from King James after the Hampton Court Conference of 1604, which brought together most of the ecclesiastical and theological leaders of the Church of England to consider the state of the Church. The New English Bible was created at the behest of the Church of Scotland, the Church of England, and the other principal protestant denominations in Great Britain. Both versions had large purposes. The Authorized Version was intended to be the only Bible read in services in all Churches of England. The New English Bible was intended to remove the language barrier between English-speaking people and the truth of the Holy Scriptures.

For both versions, the persons selected to make the translations were regarded as the most learned (or among the most learned) in the land in their knowledge of the texts and of their underlying languages, persons who were scholarly and academic in training and temperament. For both versions the primary objective of the translation was accuracy: that is to say, fidelity to the underlying texts, the Greek of the New Testament manuscripts, and the Hebrew of the Old Testament manuscripts.

For both versions, the basic method was translation and approval within a committee structure, as opposed to the long line of individuals (in English, from the version of William Tyndale in 1526 to those of J. B. Phillips in the 1950s, for example) who assumed personal responsibility for a translation. The Authorized Version had a total of about fifty translators, divided into six panels (three for the Old Testament, two for the New Testament, and one for the Apocrypha), and another group (made up of representatives of all six panels) to review and approve all of the final translations. The New English Bible had a total of about thirty translators, with one panel for the Old Testament, one for the New Testament, one for the Apocrypha, and one of literary advisers who reviewed the entire translation; the final drafts were submitted to a joint committee.

Both versions were prepared with care and deliberation. The Authorized Version was a total of seven years (1604–1611) in the making. For the New English Bible, the New Testament took fourteen years (1947–1961), and the Old Testament and the Apocrypha took twenty-three years (1947–1970).

The two versions also have some differences. The Authorized Version was not intended to be a "new" translation, but rather a drawing together of the best features of earlier translations: by reviewing those earlier translations against the underlying Greek and Hebrew, the translators said that they hoped to make one principal good one out of the many good ones of the past. They drew especially heavily on Tyndale (1526) for the New Testament, and on the Geneva Bible (1560) for the Old Testament. The language of their translation was thus already out of date (even somewhat archaic) when the Authorized Version was first published. The New English Bible, on the other hand, was intended to be a completely new translation, and not a revision of any earlier version nor a combination of any existing translations.

For the translators of the Authorized Version, the creation of an underlying text from which to work was not a major problem: at that time, the late medieval recension of the Greek called the *Textus Receptus* and the Massoretic text of the Hebrew (from 9th–11th-century copies) were considered reliable. The translators had printed texts of these, as well as polyglot versions, interlinear translations, textual commentaries, and (of course) the readings adopted for the other translations. The translators of the New

English Bible faced a more complicated textual problem. Many significant and extensive biblical manuscripts (such as the 4th-century Codex Sinaiticus) had been discovered in the meantime, and many brief but even earlier manuscripts (like the Qumran Dead Sea Scrolls, mostly from 170 B.C. to A.D. 70) were coming to light. The translators had to devote considerable attention to deciding what texts to follow, and they ended by creating an eclectic text.

There were also some tactical differences between the two versions. The translators of the Authorized Version thought that literal accuracy was paramount. They had several overseers "of the most ancient and grave divines in either of the universities" to help on words that have "divers significations." They reproduced the imagery, syntax, and conjunctions of the biblical Hebrew quite literally. And, according to John Selden, their procedure in committee was to read the proposed translation aloud to the group: the person who had done the translating of a given book would read his work aloud, and the other members of the committee would follow another text and interrupt only when they found a fault with what they had heard (*Table Talk,* Section V, par.2).

The translators seem not to have concerned themselves explicitly with what we call "style." Toward the end of their Preface, "The Translators to the Reader," they justify their flexibility in the use of words on the principle that "niceness in words was always counted the next step to trifling"—which is much like Bacon's "first distemper of learning" in the *Advancement of Learning,* "when men study words and not matter."

On the other hand, the translators of the New English Bible were given quite specific directions about the style that they should try to achieve. A memorandum from Professor C. H. Dodd, the General Director of the New English Bible, set forth these principles:

> It is to be genuinely English in idiom, such as will not awaken a sense of strangeness or remoteness. Ideally, we aim at a "timeless" English, avoiding equally both archaisms and transient modernisms. The version should be plain enough to convey its meaning to any reasonably intelligent person (so far as verbal expression goes), yet not

bald or pedestrian. It should *not* aim at preserving "hallowed associations"; it *should* aim at conveying a sense of reality. It should be as accurate as may be without pedantry. It is to be hoped that, at least occasionally, it may produce arresting and memorable renderings. It should have sufficient dignity to be read aloud. (quoted in F. F. Bruce, *The English Bible*, 2d edn., New York, Oxford, 1970, p. 237.)

As the Chairman of the Joint Committee summed it up in the Preface to each volume, the translators were asked to use "contemporary idiom" and to avoid the "traditional 'biblical' English." In the Introduction to the New Testament volume, Professor Dodd speaks as follows on behalf of the translators themselves:

In doing our work, we have constantly striven to follow our instructions and render the Greek, as we understood it, into the English of the present day, that is, into the natural vocabulary, constructions, and rhythms of contemporary speech. We have sought to avoid archaism, jargon, and all that is either stilted or slipshod.

The Preface is candid in observing that "sound scholarship does not necessarily carry with it a delicate sense of English style"; for this reason a panel of "trusted literary advisers" scrutinized everything "verse by verse, sentence by sentence" to secure "the tone and level of language appropriate to the different kinds of writing to be found in the Bible."

Perhaps the most important difference between these two versions, however, is time. They are separated by three and a half centuries—really about four centuries in language-time—and they are thus products of different eras, almost of different cultures.

The two versions offer a remarkable opportunity for comparison. It would be hard to imagine two long texts that had so much in common in their auspices, their purposes, their translators, and their procedures. In comparing passages, we can avoid ones in which the underlying texts are different. So, in interpreting their styles, we can try to see how these different worlds express themselves.

I

Whenever we are invited to compare two things that have much in common, the instinctive wish of many of us is to think about which one we prefer. This is the most essential comparison that we know how to make on a personal and emotional level. So, to begin with, we might as well compare a few familiar passages from the Authorized Version and the New English Bible to see which one we prefer. (I will modernize the spelling and punctuation of the Authorized Version throughout this chapter in order to avoid that diversion of our attention.) Here are four passages as a sort of appetizer.

1. *Psalm 23.6* (the concluding sentence)
   Authorized Version:
   Surely goodness and mercy shall follow me
   all the days of my life,
   and I will dwell in the house of the Lord for ever.

   New English Bible:
   Goodness and love unfailing, these will follow me
   all the days of my life,
   and I shall dwell in the house of the Lord my whole
   life long.

2. *Isaiah 40.3*
   Authorized Version:
   The voice of him that crieth in the wilderness,
   Prepare ye the way of the Lord,
   make straight in the desert a highway for our God.

   New English Bible:
   There is a voice that cries:
   Prepare a road for the Lord through the wilderness,
   clear a highway across the desert for our God.

3. *Matthew 6.34*
   Authorized Version:
   Take therefore no thought for the morrow,
   for the morrow shall take thought for the things of
   itself.
   Sufficient unto the day is the evil thereof.

New English Bible:

So do not be anxious about tomorrow;
tomorrow will look after itself.
Each day has troubles enough of its own.

4. *John 1.1–5*
Authorized Version:
In the beginning was the Word,
 and the Word was with God, and the Word was
 God.
The same was in the beginning with God.
All things were made by him,
 and without him was not any thing made that was
 made.
In him was life,
 and the life was the light of men.
And the light shineth in darkness,
and the darkness comprehended it not.

New English Bible:
When all things began, the Word already was.
 The Word dwelt with God, and what God was,
 the Word was.
The Word, then, was with God at the beginning,
and through him all things came to be;
 no single thing was created without him.
All that came to be was alive with his life,
 and that life was the light of men.
The light shines on in the dark,
 and the darkness has never mastered it.

It's too bad that we can't exchange, with one another, our preferences about these four passages. What would we learn if we could do so? At the least, our gut reactions. Perhaps not so sharp or slashing as T. S. Eliot's famous animadversion against the New English Bible. We are, he wrote,

entitled to expect from a panel chosen from among the most distinguished scholars of our day at least a work of dignified mediocrity. When we find that we are offered something far below that modest level, something which astonishes in its combination of the vulgar, the trivial, and the pedantic, we ask in alarm: 'What is happening to the English language?' . . . So long as the *New English Bible* was used only for private reading, it would be merely a symptom of the decay of the English language in the middle of the twentieth century. But the more it is adopted for religious services the more it will become an active agent of decadence. (London *Sunday Telegraph,* Dec. 16, 1962, p. 7)

Nor so blunt as the censure on the Authorized Version offered in 1611 to one of the king's attendants by the Hebrew scholar who hadn't been invited to be a translator, Dr. Hugh Broughton:

The late Bible . . . was sent to me to censure: which bred in me a sadness that will grieve me while I breathe, it is so ill done. Tell His Majesty that I had rather be rent in pieces with wild horses, than any such translation by my consent should be urged upon poor churches. . . . The new edition crosseth me. I require it to be burnt. (quoted in F. F. Bruce, *The English Bible,* 1970, p. 107.)

It is likely that our reactions are not so strong as either of these. We can, if we want to, say that those two were examples of prejudice. Is every preference a form of prejudice, then? Or only strong preferences? Or only preferences that are far removed from our own?

As a substitute for sharing our own reactions—or prejudices— let me tell you about the results of an informal survey that I recently made. I gave a questionnaire with the two versions of nine relatively familiar passages, like the four above, to more than fifty people and asked them which version they preferred as a piece of English prose. The people were all more than twenty-one years of age, college graduates, readers, not specialists in these matters. As you might expect, some preferred one and some the other, and only one or two preferred the same version for all passages. The Authorized Version was preferred a little more than the New English Bible, almost two-thirds of the time. Men and women had similar preferences, as did those who had and those who had not attended religious services regularly at some period in their lives, and the results were similar whether the two versions were identified or not.

What mattered most was the age of the respondents. Those over fifty preferred the Authorized Version more than three-fourths of the time. On the other hand, those under thirty preferred the New English Bible almost two-thirds of the time. With age being the most significant variable, the overall preference could therefore have been altered within the two extremes simply by increasing (or decreasing) the number of younger (or older) persons in the sample.

I cannot guarantee these results as universal truth. But what do they tell us about the group who were responding to the questionnaire? I'm not sure. I suppose the results suggest that we tend to prefer what we are more familiar with. The preference of older people for the Authorized Version may reflect familiarity, for one reason or another, with these passages or with others like them in this version sometime from childhood onward. The preference of younger people for the New English Bible suggests that the contemporary language of the New English Bible is more familiar to them—and they find it more comfortable—than the old-fashioned language of the Authorized Version.

A general preference for one version over the other is some kind of reflection of what we usually call our taste. Another way of putting it is to say that it reflects our sense of style. But at bottom our preferences—our taste, our sense of style—are a clue to our deepest identity as a human being. Hence our reading of the texts is offering to tell us truths about ourselves. For me, these truths are mysterious and hard to understand, ineffable even, in water that seems murky and bottomless. Those are fortunate to whom the text speaks clearly about these matters. But our preferences are telling us something about ourselves, whether we understand that something or not.

II

So the question is: What else are these two versions of the Bible telling us? Not: Which one is better? And not: What are the underlying Greek and Hebrew thought to mean? But: What, in fact, are these two texts telling us that is distinctive to its own version? Each version is a new text, a combination of the underlying text as the translators understood it, in an English equivalent as the translators perceived it. This new text has its own integrity and can be read for itself alone.

I would like for us to review some short passages from these two texts and see whether our understanding is different between the one and the other. For convenience, I will ask us to focus, in turn, on five features, to each of which I will devote a short section of examples. First, the choice of words; next, the relative economy of the text; then, the degree of balance of the structure; then, the degree of rhythm; and, finally, the dramatic dimensions of the discourse.

Here are a few familiar passages from the Sermon on the Mount as it is given in the Gospel According to St. Matthew. I would like for us to center our attention here on the difference in the diction of the Authorized Version (AV) and the New English Bible (NEB). The speaker in all of these examples is, of course, Jesus:

> AV: Let your light so shine before men, that they may see your good works, and glorify your Father which is in heaven. (Matthew 5.16)

> NEB: And you, like the lamp, must shed light among your fellows, so that, when they see the good you do, they may give praise to your Father in heaven.

Some comparisons of the diction of these two passages are: "men" (AV), "your fellows" (NEB); "good works" (AV), "the good you do" (NEB); "glorify" (AV), "give praise to" (NEB). Here are a couple of the Beatitudes:

> AV: Blessed are they that mourn: for they shall be comforted. (Matthew 5.4)

> NEB: How blest are the sorrowful; they shall find consolation.

> AV: Blessed are they which do hunger and thirst after righteousness: for they shall be filled. (Matthew 5.6)

> NEB: How blest are those who hunger and thirst to see right prevail; they shall be satisfied.

In the former Beatitude, the comparisons are: "they that mourn" (AV), "the sorrowful" (NEB); "be comforted" (AV), "find consolation" (NEB). In the latter: "after righteousness" (AV), "to see right prevail" (NEB); "be filled" (AV), "be satisfied" (NEB). For a final example from the Sermon on the Mount, this sentence about the beauty of the lilies of (or in) the fields:

> AV: I say unto you, That even Solomon in all his glory was not arrayed like one of these. (Matthew 6.29)

> NEB: I tell you, even Solomon in all his splendour was not attired like one of these.

The comparisons are: "I say unto you" (AV), "I tell you" (NEB); "glory" (AV), "splendour" (NEB); "arrayed" (AV), "attired" (NEB).

For one other example with the same speaker (but not from the Sermon on the Mount), this passage immediately follows Jesus' address to God and relates to his ministry on earth:

> AV: Come unto me, all ye that labor and are heavy laden, and I will give you rest. (Matthew 11.28)

> NEB: Come to me, all whose work is hard, whose load is heavy; and I will give you relief.

The main comparisons are: "ye that labor" (AV), "whose work is hard" (NEB); "are heavy laden" (AV), "whose load is heavy" (NEB); "rest" (AV), "relief" (NEB).

It is hard to generalize about all of these comparisons at once. But in these passages, the AV often seems more vague, the NEB more specific; the AV more active, the NEB more passive. The vagueness of the AV here tends to suggest dignity and elevation of the subject, while the specificity of the NEB tends to suggest the particularity of the ordinary. The active-passive comparison tends to make the AV seem more vigorous, the NEB more static.

The diction is telling us, in these passages, something about the character of Jesus in the perception of the translators. The Jesus of the AV is a character of force and dignity, and the Jesus of the NEB is one who is careful and reasonable. They are not in contrast to one another, but they are a little different from one another.

To turn to a passage about other characters, here is a description of some of Jesus' disciples after they have heard him declare that they must eat the flesh of the Son of man and drink his blood in order to have life in them:

> AV: Many therefore of his disciples, when they had heard this, said, This is a hard saying; who can hear it? (John 6.60)

> NEB: Many of his disciples on hearing it exclaimed, 'This is more than we can stomach! Why listen to such talk?'

The NEB is, of course, more particular and more idiomatic. "This is a hard saying" (AV) becomes "This is more than we can stomach" (NEB), and "who can hear it" (AV) is rendered as "Why listen to such talk?" (NEB). The disciples seem, in the AV, to be bemused and resistant; in the NEB they are shocked and disgusted.

Here is one final passage about diction. When St. Paul was arguing in the city square of Athens with casual passers-by, some Epicurean and Stoic philosophers joined issue with him.

> AV: And some said, What will this babbler say? other some, He seemeth to be a setter forth of strange gods. (Acts 17.18)

> NEB: Some said, 'What can this charlatan be trying to say?'; others, 'He would appear to be a propagandist for foreign deities.'

"The babbler" of the AV is "this charlatan" of the NEB. The "setter forth of strange gods" is "a propagandist for foreign deities" in the NEB. What is mockery in the AV is attack in the NEB, where the philosophers are also undercut by being made to speak the cant of bureaucracy.

Let me say again that we are not trying, in comparing the diction of these two translations, to determine which version is "right" or "better." These are different questions. We are trying to see what each text is telling us through its diction.

III

Like the choice of words, the degree of economy of a text usually tells us something. What are the consequences of greater or lesser economy in the use of language? We need some examples

to think about. For a simple one, the beginning of the Lord's
Prayer, with Jesus speaking:

> AV: Our Father which art in heaven,
> Hallowed be thy name. (Matthew 6.9)
> NEB: Our Father in heaven,
> thy name be hallowed.

The NEB leaves out "which art" in the first line and has a different arrangement of words in the second.

Here are two slightly longer examples, both also from Jesus'
Sermon on the Mount:

> AV: Therefore all things whatsoever ye would that men
> should do to you, do ye even so to them: for this is
> the law and the prophets. (Matthew 7.12)

> NEB: Always treat others as you would like them to treat
> you: that is the Law and the prophets.

AV is about a half longer than NEB; the expansive, sweeping
opening of the AV is, in the NEB, a succinct assertion.

> AV: Therefore I say unto you, Take no thought for your
> life, what ye shall eat, or what ye shall drink; nor yet
> for your body, what ye shall put on. Is not the life
> more than meat, and the body than raiment? (Mat-
> thew 6.25)

> NEB: Therefore I bid you put away anxious thoughts
> about food and drink to keep you alive, and clothes
> to cover your body. Surely life is more than food,
> the body more than clothes.

The NEB (which is about a quarter shorter) uses nouns with
infinitives where there had been three full clauses in the AV.

Here is a familiar short passage from St. Paul's first letter to
the Corinthians:

> AV: When I was a child, I spake as a child, I understood
> as a child, I thought as a child: but when I became a
> man, I put away childish things. (1 Cor. 13.11)

> NEB: When I was a child, my speech, my outlook, and
> my thoughts were all childish. When I grew up, I
> had finished with childish things.

The NEB is about a quarter shorter because it condenses three separate clauses into one.

For a final example on the matter of economy of language, here is a short passage from the beginning of the Book of Ecclesiastes:

> AV: One generation passeth away, and another generation cometh: but the earth abideth for ever. (Eccl. 1.4)

> NEB: Generations come and generations go, while the earth endures for ever.

The AV is about a quarter longer, mainly because it uses articles with the opening nouns. We have gone from fourteen to eleven words. Let us try to reduce the passage still further. Here is one possibility, using seven words:

> Generations pass on, but the world endures.

And here it is reduced to four words, for me the ultimate reduction:

> Generations die; earth endures.

On the other end of the scale, it would be equally possible to lengthen the AV text from its fourteen words. Here it is arbitrarily doubled in length, to exactly twenty-eight words:

> One generation spends its time on earth and then passes away; another generation follows on earth, and it too passes away. Only the earth itself lasts for ever.

The process of lengthening could be continued, I suppose, for as long as your energy held out.

In a basic conceptual sense, the essential message has remained about the same in the several permutations of this text, and of the earlier one from First Corinthians and the three before that from the Sermon on the Mount.

But the texts have not been telling us the same thing. So far as the AV and the NEB texts go, I have chosen examples in which the AV is a little longer in order to provide a common basis for discussion. Of course it is what is done with the length that counts in these two versions. I would like to limit the generalizations to the particular examples I have cited and not try to talk about the versions as a whole.

What, in these examples, is the AV text telling us that is different from what the NEB text is telling us? Conceptually, very little. But emotionally, they may be telling us a great deal that is different from one another. In the passage from Ecclesiastes, for example, the issue is our emotional understanding of the transiency of life—including our own life—when set against the relative permanence of the earth. The structure and solemnity of the AV create a sense of inevitability and make an impact on us: as if to say, here is something you must take to heart for your own understanding of your self. The structure and tone of the NEB also suggest a sense of inevitability, but of a more casual cast: as if to say, that's the way things are, here today and gone tomorrow.

The AV examples tend as a group to proceed, with their slightly greater length, in a leisurely manner and with notable dignity. Through their manner, they seem to be leading us to the belief that what they are saying has unusual importance for us and that they deserve our undivided attention. The NEB examples proceed, with their slightly lesser length, in a straightforward, assertive manner. Through their manner, they seem to be telling us that their message is entirely and sincerely true.

IV

Let me offer a few examples that illustrate different degrees of balance in the structure of sentences. Here is a simple one from St. Paul's speech before the Court of the Areopagus in Athens, as to why we should seek the Lord:

AV: for in him we live, and move, and have our being. (Acts 17.28)

NEB: for in him we live and move, in him we exist.

The balance in the former is carried through each of the three verbs; in the latter, the balance is changed with a different form of structure for the third verb.

Here is a slightly different kind of balance. St. Paul is again the speaker, expounding his truth about God to the Romans:

AV: What shall we then say to these things? If God be for
us, who can be against us? (Romans 8.31)

NEB: With all this in mind, what are we to say? If God
is on our side, who is against us?

The balance in the former example consists in the verbal contrast
of "for us" in opposition to "against us," while in the latter example the structure of "on our side" as opposed to "against us"
does not use verbal contrast.

Here is another form of balance, dependent on word play. It
is part of the narrative, in Mark, of Jesus healing a boy with an
unclean spirit:

AV: And straightway the father of the child cried out, and
said with tears, Lord, I believe; help thou my unbelief. (Mark 9.24)

NEB: 'I have faith,' cried the boy's father; 'help me where
faith falls short.'

The force of the former is based on the paradox of "I believe"
and "my unbelief"; in the latter, contrast is hardly noticed in the
comparison of "faith" on the one hand and of "faith falls short"
on the other.

I will put this passage from Mark into a kind of performance
structure to emphasize the balance; in it, Jesus is foretelling his
death:

AV: For what shall it profit a man if he shall
gain the whole world, and
lose his own soul? (Mark 8.36)

NEB: What does a man gain by
winning the whole world
at the cost of his true self?

The former used the balanced contrast of "gain" and "lose,"
while the latter has no balance of that sort.

For a final example, here is a familiar passage from the Sermon on the Mount put into performance structure:

AV: Lay not up for your selves treasures upon earth,
where moth and rust doth corrupt, and
where thieves break through, and steal.

> But lay up for your selves treasures in heaven,
> where neither moth nor rust doth corrupt, and
> where thieves do not break through, nor steal.
>   (Matthew 6.19–20)

> NEB: Do not store up for yourselves treasures on earth,
> where it grows rusty and moth-eaten, and
> thieves break in to steal it.
> Store up treasure in heaven,
> where there is no moth and no rust to spoil it,
> no thieves to break in and steal.

Notice the intricate care with which the structure is balanced in the former example: two sentences in exact parallel with one another, down to small details. In the latter example, the deviations from the exactitude of the parallelism are clear by comparison.

Balance (or partial balance, or lack of balance) of the sort for which I have been offering examples intimates to us as readers something about the way that writers perceive the subject about which they are writing. On the one hand, a perception that the subject is clear, orderly, and understandable: this is the direction toward which AV examples are pointing. On the other hand, among many other possibilities, a perception that the subject is difficult, intricate, or perplexing: this is the direction toward which the NEB examples are pointing. It is not a matter of which is right and which is wrong: either could be argued for. It is a matter of how the translators write about their subject from the way they perceive it and accordingly how we are led to understand it.

V

The impact on us that comes from the balance (or lack of balance) of a discourse is paralleled by the impact on us that comes from the rhythm (or lack of rhythm) of the language, its verbal music. The Bible is full of the verbal music of songs. The Psalms, the Song of Songs, Lamentations, Job, Proverbs, a good deal of the writings of the Prophets, and poems scattered through the other books, like the verses known as the Magnificat and the Benedictus in the Gospel According to St. Luke (1.46–55 and 1.68–79).

Since the music of poetry involves questions which we aren't discussing, I will limit the few examples I can offer to passages of prose. From them, we can try to see what the rhythm is telling us.

For a start, consider the familiar beginning of the thirteenth chapter of St. Paul's first letter to the Corinthians. I will put this and all the following passages into very simple performance structures and mark the stresses according to my reading of them, in the manner I used in chapter 4 above.

AV: Though I spéak with the tóngues of mén and of ángels,
    and háve nòt chárity,
    Ì am becòme as sóunding bráss,
    or a tínkling cýmbal. (1 Cor. 13.1)

NEB: I may spéak in tóngues of mén or of ángels,
    but if Í am without lóve,
    Í am a sóunding góng
    or a clánging cýmbal.

This is a smooth, moderately light, rhythmical passage. The smoothness comes from the mixture of the large number of two-syllable time-lapses with one-syllable time-lapses between stresses. The beat is heavy only where special emphasis falls on the state to be abhorred: "háve nòt chárity" or "without lóve."

The two versions are about equal in the lightness of their beat. A good hint about the relative lightness or heaviness of the rhythm of a passage can be arrived at by calculating the proportion of stresses to syllables in the passage and by comparing it with those of other passages. I have done this calculation for the passages I will quote, and for many, many others. The range is from about one and a half syllables per stress (a very heavy, dense rhythm) to about three and a half syllables per stress (an extremely light, racing rhythm), with the average of about two and a half syllables per stress. On the average, the rhythm of the Authorized Version is a little lighter than that of the New English Bible. Since I think these results merit no claim to mathematical precision, I will refer to these results only with passages where they seem clearly significant.

Here is another passage in which gracefulness may likewise seem, at first glance, to be the main characteristic of the rhythm.

It is from the Book of Ruth, part of the answer that Ruth makes
to her mother-in-law Naomi upon being urged to leave her and
go home now that Naomi's husband and both of her sons are
dead:

> AV: Entréat me nót to léave thèe,
>   or to retúrn from fóllowing áfter thèe:
>   for whìther thóu gòest, Í will go:
>   and whère thóu lòdgest, Í will lodge:
>   thy peòple shall be mý peòple,
>   and thy Gòd mý Gòd:
>   whère thóu dièst, wìll Í diè,
>   and thére wìll Í be búried. (Ruth 1.16–17)

> NEB: Dò nót úrge mè to go báck and desért yòu.
>   Whère yóu gò, Í will go,
>   and whère yóu stày, Í will stay.
>   Yóur pèople shall be my pèople,
>   and yóur Gòd my Gòd.
>   Whère yóu dìe, Í will die,
>   and thére Í will be búried.

My impression is that the more usual reading of this passage is
much lighter and more rhythmical, with the most familiar lines,
for example, read (or, as I think, misread) somewhat as follows:

> fŏr whíthĕr thŏu góešt, Í wĭll gŏ;
> aňd whére thŏu lódgĕst, Í wĭll lŏdge: (AV)

Such a rhythm would indeed create a graceful, poetic effect, with
its mixture of anapests and iambs, but it fails to put the main
emphasis on the *thou-I* juncture and the secondary emphasis on
their joint action.

The rhythm, as I have given it—based on the internal logic
of the passage—is quite heavy, much heavier, for example, than
in the passage from First Corinthians. (The proportion of syllables to stresses here is near the minimum among all the passages I have examined, and hence among the heaviest.) The
rhythm adds a force to Ruth's speech that puts her plans beyond
dispute. Her speech offers a rhythmic picture of a mind that is

made up, a portrait of a very strong woman appropriate to be the grandmother of Jesse and great grandmother of the great King David.

It is worth noticing why the rhythm of the Authorized Version is, in this passage, a little less heavy than that of the New English Bible. The normal language of the Authorized Version is more highly inflected and has more polysyllabic particles: "whither thou goest" as opposed to "where you go," for example; the additional syllables, without stress, lighten the rhythm by increasing the proportion of syllables to stresses.

There is a lot of variation in the music of prose. Here, in a passage from First Kings, the king of Israel orders the prophet Micaiah to be thrown into prison for having given him an unfavorable prediction:

> AV: Pút this féllow in the príson,
> and féed him with bréad of afflíction
> and with wáter of afflíction,
> untìl Í cóme in péace. (1 Kings 22.27)

> NEB: Lóck this féllow ùp,
> and gíve him príson diet of bréad and wáter
> untìl Í come home in sáfety.

(The king was killed in the battle and did not "come home in safety," but we aren't told what happened to the languishing prophet.) The rhythm is rough rather than heavy in both versions of this passage, conveying the peremptoriness of the order. It is notably rough in the New English Bible version, in which there are only one-syllable time-lapses between the stresses.

This is a short passage from the Parable of the Vineyard. Please consider what the rhythm is telling us about the workmen who are speaking:

> AV: Thèse lást have wróught but óne hóur,
> and thóu hast màde thém èqual ùnto ús,
> which have bórne the búrden and héat of the dáy.
> (Matthew 20.12)

> NEB: Thèse late-comers have done ònly óne hóur's wórk,
> yet yóu have pùt thém on a lével with ús,
> who have swéated the whóle dày lóng in the blázing sún!

In both versions, the workmen are clearly displeased at the way they have been treated by the owner of the vineyard. There is no substantial difference in the purport of the two versions, but there is a difference in the nuances because of the rhythm. In the New English Bible, the rhythm is firmer and stronger: compare "onlȳ óne hóur's wórk" with "bŭt óne hóur" in the Authorized Version, or "tħe whóle dày lóng iň tħe blázïng sún" (NEB) with "tħe búrdĕn aňd héat ŏf tħe dáy" (AV). In the Authorized Version, the workmen are represented as feeling put upon and irritated, while in the New English Bible they are aggrieved and angry.

For one final example of rhythm, here is a passage from Jesus' Sermon on the Mount:

> AV: Júdge nót, that ẏe be not júdged.
> For with whát júdgment ẏe júdge,
> ẏe shall be júdged:
> and with whát méasure yé méte,
> it shall be méasured to yóu agáin. (Matthew 7.1–2)

> NEB: Páss nó júdgement, and yóu will nót be júdged.
> For as yóu júdge óthers,
> sò yóu wíll yoursélves be júdged,
> and whátever méasure you deal out to óthers
> will be déalt báck to yóu.

This is a strong, assertive message in both versions. It is full of imperatives, and the discourse is bearing down on the reader to impress us with the importance of this truth. The Authorized Version is a trifle blunter. It has more stresses and less separation between stresses, and hence a heavier rhythm. Compare: "Júdge nót, thăt yé be not júdged" (AV) and "Páss nó júdgemĕnt, ănd yóu wíll nót bĕ júdged" (NEB); or "wĭth whát méasŭre yé méte" (AV) and "whátĕvĕr méasŭre yŏu deal out tŏ óthĕrs" (NEB). As a consequence, the speech in the Authorized Version seems more fiery and frightening and that in the New English Bible more calm and reasonable.

VI

The dramatic dimensions of a discourse affect our understanding of the text. Sometimes the drama depends on the relations of the writer and the reader, and sometimes on the human action portrayed or implied by the text. Always what counts is our human reaction to what is being acted out in front of us. Let me offer a few examples where the Authorized Version and the New English Bible are telling us something a little different from one another because of the difference in dramatic presentation.

Here is a simple example from the Psalms:

> AV: O give thanks unto the Lord, for he is good:
> for his mercy endureth for ever. (Psalm 107.1)

> NEB: It is good to give thanks to the Lord,
> for his love endures for ever.

The Authorized Version, an exhortation, is the more dramatic of the two. We are asked to do something and are told why we should do it. The New English Bible, an assertion, is the less dramatic of the two. We are told what is a desirable course of action in general and why it is desirable. How we react depends, in part, of course, on how we naturally react to exhortations or assertions. But differently.

Here is a somewhat similar example, from the Sermon on the Mount, the conclusion to Jesus' teaching about love for our enemies:

> AV: Be ye therefore perfect, even as your Father which is
> in heaven is perfect. (Matthew 5.48)

> NEB: There must be no limit to your goodness, as your
> heavenly Father's goodness knows no bounds.

The Authorized Version is more imperative and more extravagant, while the New English Bible is more assertive and more reasonable. It is as if two slightly different kinds of personalities were speaking to us, and we react in accordance with our own personality.

But a central point about these two examples is that the Authorized Version is in the personal tradition, with a clearer sense of a discourse between two people, a speaker and a listener, and hence human involvement by the reader in the action. The New English Bible, on the other hand, is in these two examples more in the impersonal tradition, with less sense of a speaker and a listener, and hence less human involvement on the part of the reader in the action.

Here is an example of a more dramatic situation. This is Mary's response to the angel Gabriel after he has told her that she will bear Jesus:

> AV: And Mary said, Behold the handmaid of the Lord; be it unto me according to thy word. (Luke 1.38)

> NEB: 'Here am I,' said Mary; 'I am the Lord's servant; as you have spoken, so be it.'

There is a little difference in the dramatic action in these two texts. In the Authorized Version, the acceptance is all in the imperative, and Mary is made to appear more active in her acceptance and hence a little more willing. In the New English Bible, the acceptance is mainly in the form of an assertion, and Mary is made to appear more passive in her acceptance and hence perhaps a little less willing. The message to us is accordingly a bit different in the two versions.

Here is another dramatic example related to Mary. After the angel has told Mary that she will bear Jesus, Mary goes to the hill country to visit her cousin Elizabeth, who is pregnant with John the Baptist. Mary greets Elizabeth:

> AV: And it came to pass, that, when Elisabeth heard the salutation of Mary, the babe leaped in her womb; and Elisabeth was filled with the Holy Ghost: and she spake out with a loud voice, and said, Blessed art thou among women, and blessed is the fruit of thy womb. (Luke 1.41–42)

> NEB: And when Elizabeth heard Mary's greeting, the baby stirred in her womb. Then Elizabeth was filled with the Holy Spirit and cried aloud, 'God's blessing is on you above all women, and his blessing is on the fruit of your womb.'

The dramatic difference between the two versions is, I think, clear though not great. The Authorized Version is more enthusiastic, with its two imperatives in Elizabeth's cry and the baby leaping rather than stirring, while the New English Bible is in the form of a sincere assertion. For most of us, our attitude toward the forthcoming birth depends in part on our understanding of this little dramatic situation.

Here are two versions of Jesus' baptism:

> AV: And Jesus, when he was baptized, went up straightway out of the water: and, lo, the heavens were opened unto him, and he saw the Spirit of God descending like a dove, and lighting upon him: and lo, a voice from heaven, saying, This is my beloved Son, in whom I am well pleased. (Matthew 3.16–17)

> NEB: After baptism Jesus came up out of the water at once, and at that moment heaven opened; he saw the Spirit of God descending like a dove to alight upon him; and a voice from heaven was heard saying, 'This is my Son, my Beloved, on whom my favour rests.'

The Authorized Version proceeds with the air of recounting a miracle—"lo, the heavens were opened" and "lo, a voice from heaven"—while the New English Bible is more businesslike in reporting an event—"at that moment heaven opened" and "a voice from heaven was heard." And the climax—God's words—conveys a little more passion in the Authorized Version, with its strongly stressed last two words.

For a final example, here is the story of Peter's deliverance from the prison in Judea in which Herod the King had cast him:

> AV: And, behold, the angel of the Lord came upon him, and a light shined in the prison: and he smote Peter on the side, and raised him up, saying, Arise up quickly. And his chains fell off from his hands. And the angel said unto him, Gird thyself, and bind on thy sandals. And so he did. And he saith unto him, Cast thy garment about thee, and follow me. (Acts 12.7–8)

> NEB: All at once an angel of the Lord stood there, and the cell was ablaze with light. He tapped Peter on the shoulder and woke him. 'Quick! Get up!,' he

said, and the chains fell away from his wrists. The angel then said to him, 'Do up your belt and put your sandals on.' He did so. 'Now wrap your cloak round you and follow me.'

The Authorized Version is somewhat more dramatic. It begins (in the personal tradition) with an address to the reader—"And, behold, the angel of the Lord came upon him"—where the New English Bible starts with an assertion—"All at once an angel of the Lord stood there." In one, the angel "smote Peter on the side," in the other he "tapped Peter on the shoulder." In one, the angel speaks with formality and dignity: "Arise up quickly . . . gird thyself, and bind on thy sandals"; in the other, the angel speaks with the informality of a roommate: "Quick! Get up! . . . Do up your belt and put your sandals on." In short, the two accounts give a somewhat different sense of the happenings, of the characters, and of the relation between them.

There is, naturally, a consistency in the style of the Authorized Version and (on the other hand) in the style of the New English Bible. Each of these styles gives us a somewhat different understanding of its text. Let me say once more that I do not think that one of these understandings is "righter" than the other one. I have not been speaking in favor of or against either of these versions: each is the text that its translators created, with its own special qualities.

The special qualities that characterize the passages I have quoted probably characterize, in a more general way, their versions as a whole. Each version presumably draws its deep qualities from the culture and the literary tradition within which the text was created.

The version of 1611 seems to me to be, for example, more given to metaphor, while the version of our own century seems more given to abstraction. Two worlds, two cultures are speaking in their own ways, through their own styles. What this simple observation suggests is a culture in 1611 more in tune with imaginative perception (poetry?) than our more recent past was.

A comparison of the two versions may be made to reveal many things of greater or less importance about our two cultures. I am content to rest with the conclusion that these two translations of the Bible, so similar in genesis and procedure, give us different understandings, one from the other, when we focus on their styles. And that we come to a fuller understanding of any text through interpreting its style.

INDEX